MODERN PROFESSIONAL COOKERY

MODERN PROFESSIONAL COOKERY

Dr. B.K. CHAKRAVARTI

Department of Hotel Management & Catering Technology
Birla Institute of Technology (Deemed University)
Mesra, Ranchi (India)
and
Principal (Retd.), IHM, Patna
Sr Faculty, IHM, Kolkata
Visiting Faculty, University of Calcutta

AMAN PUBLICATIONS
NEW DELHI

Published by
Rajiv Jain for Aman Publications
LG-4A, Ganpati Bhawan,
4675-B/21, Ansari Road,
Darya Ganj, Delhi - 110002
PH: 23255012, 23282127
E-mail: sshjbs@yahoo.com

First Published 2010

ISBN–81–8204–053-1

ISBN–978-81–8204–053-3

SOLE DISTRIBUTOR
JINDAL BOOK SERVICES
LG-4A, Ganpati Bhawan,
4675-B/21, Ansari Road,
Darya Ganj, Delhi - 110002

Jacket Designed by :
S.M. Graphics

Printed by:
Balaji Offset, Delhi, India

Preface

Catering education and particularly education and training in food preparation, Culinary arts, Chef's training etc have been institutionalized and hundreds of young boys and girls are now going for this education by choice in numerous catering institutes/culinary institutes throughout the country.

Needless to say that, they still very much depend on limited classroom inputs and for resource materials, they depend on expensive books published mainly in USA, U.K., and Australia.

My attempt to compile a new volume handy and suitable for the new entrants of food preparation profession, will be of immense value and as an important guide and reference. Efforts are made to incorporate latest information, methodologies and steps of work in kitchens. Other useful skills to become employable worker in various ecateries and similar work place have been detailed out in the volume.

I hope, students and teachers in particular will benefit from this latest indispensable volume.

Dr. B.K. CHAKRAVARTI

Acknowledgements

I am debited to my colleagues and friends in Hotel Management & Catering Technology Department, Birla Institute of Technology, Mesra, for their help and guidance in preparing the manuscript.

I am particularly grateful to VC, E BIT, Prof H.C. Pandey and VC, BIT, Prof. P.K. Barhai for providing me the opportunity to carry on research and academic activities in the campus of BIT, Mesra.

I also thank various publishers, namely M/s Jindal Publications, M/s APH Publishing House and M/s CBS, New Delhi for providing reference materials.

I am grateful to M/s Niagra Mohak Co. USA, NIN, Hyderabad for providing and allowing useful data and references for incorporation in this book.

Thanks are due to Mr. Rajeev Jain and Mr. Sanjeev Jain for taking up this volume for publication.

Dr. B.K. CHAKRAVARTI

Contents

1

History of Kitchens

Kitchens have been the heart of the existence of mankind for many thousand years, but sadly there are no significant remains left to give the historic picture of ordinary life, in homes, where cooking, living and even sleeping all went on in the same room.

The rapid progress in technology during the course of the last centuries has affected and changed the kitchen more than any room in the house. These progressive changes were usually the result of the change in the type of fuel used and the availability of labour.

THE EARLIEST KITCHENS

Historians say that 75,000 years ago, it was more through an accident that the process of cooking was discovered. The roasted chunk of meat, which was inadvertently dropped into the fire, proved tastier and tender. This discovery prompted humans to conduct experiments on food ever since. The first cooking pot was large stone with a hollow in the middle, and the hollow was filled with water—food boiled by adding to stones. Utensils and reusable containers came later.

Cultivation of foodgrains and domestication of animals made the next turning point. As early civilizations established themselves in the fertile lands in the near East. Central America and South East Asia, life changed form a nomadic hunting and gathering existence to a more settled state where farming developed and animals were kept for their resources of milk, meat as well as skin and wool.

Egyptians were the first to discover how to make leavened bread, they also used salt as preservative. At the height of their civilization, cooking had progressed a long way form the subsistence level.

Romans were the true forerunners of the kitchen, as cooking was more varied and sophisticated and their kitchens were well equipped with utensils and ingredients. Early Roman kitchens were located in the atrium, where smoke form the fire could escape without risk. Later when atrium became the living area, the kitchen was relegated to a separate back-room. The poor lived in crowded tenements where the risk of fire was great and they depended more on food cooked in community cook shops. Charcoal was mostly used as a fuel. The Mediterranean climate made quick methods of cooking infinitely preferable to burning large fires that threw off an uncomfortable heat. Basic cooking implements found in a Roman kitchen changed little over succeeding centuries. The principle of the double boiler was discovered by the Roman and there was also a type of 'bain - marie', an open vessel in which separate jars of different foods could simmer simultaneously without mingling the tastes.

THE DARK AGES

Little is known about this age; It is generally assumed that the life had returned to a basic, brutal level, where the rigours of survival replaced the cultivation of taste.

In Northern Europe cooking was carried out over a central fore fuelled by logs, fallen branches or peat. Smoke escaped as best it could through the roof. Naturally, since most buildings were made of timber, there was a great risk of fire. The blazing heat of wood fire limited cooking methods. Most people survived in whatever could be boiled up in a cauldron kept simmering on the hearth. Since, fire was rarely allowed to go out, such broth could be kept simmering for days. A slab of bread or trencher served as an edible plate.

Baking was done alongside the fire of the central hearth due to the religious impact an abstinence form certain items of food, particularly meat, attention was diverted towards all kinds of cultivation, from growing medicinal herbs to tending vineyards and keeping bees.

THE MEDIEVAL KITCHENS

Despite improvements in agriculture, central hearths were still common and basic diet remained grains, beans or cabbage, supplemented by occasional fresh meat or fish. With the increase of population, which was concentrated in towns, market trading cook shops for meat, and bakeries where home-made dough could be baked into bread became very popular. Food poisoning from decaying produce and epidemics brought on by contaminated water was the major problem.

When stone began to replace timber as a building material, the hall of the house was transformed. Gradually, in castles, abbeys and fortresses, fire places were set into the wall with ovens frequently build in alongside, sharing the same flue. Kitchen was now adjacent to the great hall or else in a separate building altogether to minimise the fire risk and exclude the smoke and odours of roasting meat. This stage marked the beginning of the segregation of the kitchen form the main living area.

Cooking was a communal affair, surrounding the kitchen were numerous specialized chamber for baking, brewing and storing spices, wine and grain. Herb gardens, ponds, stocked with fresh fish, dairies, hives, vineyards and orchards kept communities of several hundred people self sufficient from one season to the next.

Spices had been rediscovered by the crusaders once again played a vital role in making unreliable or monotonous food palatable. For the rich, cooking began to regain the sophistication of classical times, with the number of dishes on the table and the variety of spices they contained being the indication of wealth and status. State bread trenchers were being replaced by wooden plates, but people still used their fingers for eating as there were no forks in common use for centuries to come.

NEW HORIZON

During the following few centuries, people were more concerned about comfort and started living in manor houses which were as self-sufficient but less communally organized, unlike fortified castles.

The main problem was how to regulate the heat of open fire and cook easily, since the fire could not be turned down. Most changes in the kitchen technology form twelfth to seventeenth century concentrated mainly on this problem. Various devices were developed to vary the distance of the pot form the flame for quicker or slower heating. Ratchet and chain system was evolved, which enabled pots and kettle to be swung over the fire at different levels, 'idle backs' allowed kettles to be titled for pouring without burning the fingers, while the flat bottom pans were set on trivets.

Another seventeenth century innovation was the dresser, which evolved from a flat board fixed to the wall where tasters checked the food for poison before it was offered to the master. From the flat board with shelves above, the dresser developed into a single item of furniture with a solid back, extending to the full height of the room. Enclosed cupboards at the base were used to store linen with plates displaced above. By the end of the eighteenth century timber stocks in Northern Europe had been seriously depleted, in England laws were passed which permitted only certain types of wood to be burned. The rural poor were allowed to collect dead wood for their open hearths. Elsewhere, coal began to take over. The industrial revolution speeded up the pace of kitchen development. The central innovation was the close range or kitchener, an enclosed iron stove which allowed better regulation of heat and more economical use of fuel.

The kitchen played an important role in reflecting the status of the people. Except in cottages or simple homes of the poor where everything largely happened in one room, kitchen was no longer an integrated part of the household. It was now the domain of the army of domestic servants, employed for cooking, cleaning and running the homes. Women of the house selfdom interfered in the kitchen activities, except to consult the cook on the day's menu or intervene problems, in the middle class terraced house, the kitchen was a less hospitable place, it was usually located in the discolouration caused by coal fires and gas lightning. Floors were stone flagged or quarry tiled to withstand daily scrubbing, a scullery for washing was a nineteenth century addition to the basic kitchen, reflecting the increased appreciation of the role of hygiene and health.

INDIAN KITCHENS

The Indian tradition is like no others, in the past, an inextricable part of this tradition had been the joint family system from which steamed a distinct architecture. Large family rooms, courtyards, and a kitchen that not only catered to a large faculty, but in a typical situation, was the nucleus of the household.

The courtyard in the Indian houses have always been main core of the houses, hub of activity, where sleeping, eating, and gossiping takes places. Since the type of Indian cooking needs considerable space for bulk storage and preparation, kitchens are allocated to a part of the house, i.e., courtyard. Moreover, main water source like borewells, etc., are always located in the courtyard.

Indian cooking is such that everything that was needed or consumed had to be made at home. That involves a lot of storage for grains and spices which could be very conveniently done near the cooking space. Baskets woven from twine and leaves were the containers for grain. Grain and spices were washed and dried in the courtyard before use. Fresh grinding of grain and spices was done before each meal, which also needed space.

Wood was the major source of fuel, cooking was done over an open fire *(angeethi)*. Before liquefied petroleum, kerosene and electric stoves were invented, twigs of wood and coconut husks provided effective fuel. Storage for fuel-firewood stoves, charcoal ovens was to be provided adjacent to the courtyard. Every night, when day's cooking was done, a coat of cow dung was applied to the angeethi to ready and distinct it for the next day's use. Tall chimneys were provided above the angeethi or stove through which the fumes could be exhausted out.

As per the Indian traditions, cooking as well as eating is done while sitting on floor, thus the kitchens were also designed accordingly - the cooking stove was placed on·the floor. All the ingredients needed for cooking need to be stored within the reach of the cook, while sitting.

In the days before the steel invasion, utensils were made of three basic metals: brass, copper and iron.

But with the great waves of immigrants form European countries that pored into the country, new customs and types of food were introduced and Indian cooking began to acquire its variety some families, started eating on the dining table adjacent to the kitchen. Post-independence kitchens have more of British influence with standing kitchen becoming more popular in the urban area. The concept of kitchen has totally changed due to technological advancement and the globalisation as the new range of labour- saving products are available in the market, now kitchen planning is greatly influenced by the personality of the user, individual style and requirement, level of income and standard of living.

These kitchens stood out because of their sheer size, use of locally available materials, their non challenge to aesthetics and subtle rustic appeal. Now these cooking spaces have given way to the modular, practical variety, best suited to a modern life style.

KITCHEN TECHNOLOGY

Many of the labour- saving devices that have transformed the kitchen in modern times were first envisaged in the late nineteenth century. The principle of artificial refrigeration was discovered in the 1870s. The gas stove made its first appearance in 1850s but it was another 50 years before the common people overcame their suspicions and began to adopt it. The pressure cooker also appeared during the period.

Early domestic gadgets such as miners, mixers and grinders were cumbersome and difficult to operate, and only when the small electric motor was developed in the 1920s did these ideas become practical for daily use in the average kitchen. Electrification and the rise in gas consumption have changed the kitchens to a great extent.

The average Indian urban kitchen had been through the transformation only during the last few decades.

KITCHEN REQUIREMENTS

Kitchen, the nerve centre of a home, is the hub of its activities and is the room in any house that is used the most, each day. It can prove a place of boredom and monotony. Alternatively, it is well planned and laid out, it can turn out to be a very important room, where one can look for a serene, reposeful and cheerful atmosphere. Hygiene, and cleanliness in a kitchen must be maintained at all costs and on all occasion. Designing a kitchen is a subjective matter—more so to suit temperament and pocket.

The first step towards kitchen designing is to frame out the requirement of the user. Cooking is not a single activity, but a series of related tasks, each with its own specific demands in terms of space, equipment, and fitting,

Marshalling these separate functions into a smoothly coordinated activity leads to the ideal kitchen. The total requirement of the kitchen can be divided into various work zones or centres. Basically, five work centres are essential in any kitchen, with two optional centres.

REFRIGERATOR AND FOOD STORAGE CENTRE

Food storage in the kitchen can be divided into perishable and nonperishable items. Perishable food items take their place in the refrigerator or deep freezer. Perishable items include fresh vegetable frozen food, meat, canned food, etc. Non perishable items include - sugar, tea flour pulses, rice, sauces, spices, vegetables like onions, potatoes, etc. Storage for cold drinks bottles is also provided near the refrigerator. Deep freezers are also kept in this centres. The space needed for food storage and the capacity of fridge and freezer depends on the size of the family, the shopping habits and the life style. Eight cubic feet of refrigerator space is the minimum recommended for two people; add a cubic foot for each additional family member and two extra feet if there are frequent guests at home. Power for refrigerator or deep freezer is also provided in this zone. If separate deep freezer is needed, three or four square feet of freezer space for each person in the family is a good yardstick.

Refrigerators higher than the work top level are usually placed at the ends of counter runs, so that they do not interrupt the flow of the work for which the countries are utilized.

SINK AND CLEANUP CENTRE

This is the most frequently used place in the kitchen, where washing of utensils and pulses take place. The sink can be single, double or one and half bowl depending on the space and the use. The provision of dishwasher is needed here. Normally, dishwashers are placed left of the sink area for a right handed user, but it should depend on the convenience of the user. It is best to locate the sink and clean up centre between the refrigerator and the cooking area. The storage of saucepans, pots, etc. is needed near the sink or dishwasher, so that the utensils can be conveniently stored after washing, other items needed near the sink are waste disposer which is installed under the sink and water purifier geyser and water storage, etc., above the sink. Electric points and switches for water disposer, geyser and water purifier are also needed to be provide at convenient locations. Cleaning material should also be placed near the sink for an easy access. A large variety of bins and pullouts are available for cleaning supplies in the sink areas.

Sinks are usually preferred under the window, but never in the corner, the waste disposers are operated on 15 ampere electrical point beneath the sink; and a switch preferable be placed above the kitchen platform for easy access.

RANGE AND COOKING CENTRE

This is the place where main cooking takes place. There are many types of cook tops—gas stove with two, three or four burners, electric oil or hot plate, and cooking range. If the gas stove is used, a place for gas cylinder is needed under the counter. Although microwave is often considered as a part of the cooking centre, some prefer it near refrigerator or in the serving centre.

The cooking unit should be placed where steam and fumes can be easily extracted, but never under a window where fluttering curtains may catch fire. The placement of cook top is preferred along the external wall, making it easy to install an efficiently ventilation system unless and island with a hood is provided. The cook top should neither be placed under any wall cabinet nor in the corner for convenient and safe cooking

FOOD PREPARATION AND CHOPPING CENTRE

This auxiliary centre is ideally located between the refrigerator and the sink. The activities involved in this zone are cutting, chopping and pre-preparation of the food. Food storage of pulses, flour, rice, spices, onions and potatoes is needed in this zone. The equipment like food processor, mixer grinder, etc. shall be placed here. Electric points and switches for the food processor and mixer grinder are also needed near the equipment.

SERVING CENTRE

This optional work centre is located between the range and sink, if possible. This centre is used for keeping cooked food. Hot pots and pans need to be placed here. Everyday dishes, glassware, flatware, serving plates and bowls, as well as napkins and placements belong in this area. A majority of people prefer placing microwaves and ovens in this area.

EATING CENTRE AND DRINKING AREA.

This is optional centre, provided in the form of an island or peninsula. This centre can overlap with the chopping centre. Microwave or ovens can be placed in this area, along with the crockery, cutlery, kitchen lines, etc., Normally it is provided near the serving centre.

STORAGE CENTRE

In the Indian style cooking, considerable amount of storage space for grains, pulses, sugar, rice, etc., is required. The common practice is to get the weekly or monthly supplies of all these items which are kept in the food preparation centre. However, a separate space is needed for bulk storage either within the kitchen or adjacent to the kitchen. Space should be provided for large containers and for the storage of items which are not frequently used. Upper parts of the walls cabinets can be used for this purpose.

KITCHEN SINKS AND FAUCETS

No kitchen component does more jobs more often than the sink. Here's where most meals begin and end, with many a side trip during the cooking and serving processes.

Selecting a sink based on function, space and style is the best way to ensure that using it never becomes a drudgery. One can have one, two or three bowls depending on the work habits, available space and budget, with sinks, simple design and bigger size often makes a better choice. Today's sink is a multi-task centre and double- even triple bowl designs re now the norm. Single- bowl sinks are streamlined and flexible., room enough for oversize pans and cutting boards, identical twin basins simplify washing and rinsing dishes and food preparation and good for simultaneous work, a sink with one small and one large bowl is sensible for most of the household. It does not occupy much of a space while still allowing the secondary tasks to go on.

Good drainers are only slightly sloped and without grooves which collect dirt and are useless on a shallow incline so that the surface can double as a worktop.

A sink should cleanse and inspire. Place sink as close to the worktop level as possible.

Available varieties of sinks have one, two or three bowls, with or without attached drain boards. Most have predrilled holes for faucets, sprayers, soap or hot water dispensers or air gaps.

Self-rimming sinks with moulded overlaps are supported by the edge of the counter-top cutout; flush deck- mounted sinks have surrounding metal strips to hold the basin to the counter-tops, unrimmed sinks are recessed under the counter-top opening and held in place by clips. Integral bowl sinks are also available.

SINK MATERIALS

Common sink materials include stainless steel, enameled cast iron and steel, vitreous china, brass and copper, acrylic, marble stone chips (terrazzo).

STAINLESS STEEL

Stainless steel sinks come in 18 to 20 gauge (18 gauge is stronger) and in either matte or mirror finish. Chromium/ nickel blends – such as type 304 stainless steel are good. These are the only true "stainless" sinks; cheaper grades will stain. Matte finishes are much easier to keep looking clean than mirrored, and they mark scratches better. Stainless steel is relatively noisy; stainless steel sinks are light in weight. Easy to install, stain resistant and durable, the stainless steel sinks are available in single bowl, double bowl or triple bowl, with or without drain board and with various arrangements. These sinks are also available with special basket type choke stop strainer which looks and collects water in bowl to clean vegetables, utensils, etc. Sinks with integral drain boards and waste disposers are also available.

Normally, stainless steel kitchen sinks are made of, Salem stainless steel of ISI 304, 18 gauges.

ENAMELLED, CAST IRON/STEEL

Enamelled cast iron sinks are available in a variety of colours. Enamelled cast iron sinks have a heavier layer of baked on enamel than steel, making them quieter and less likely to chip, but also more expensive.

VITREOUS CHINA

Vitreous china sinks are very easy to clean and are unaffected by acids and alkalis used in the kitchen, these sinks are heavy, but can crack with heavy use.

INTEGRAL SOLID SURFACE SINKS

Today's solid surface counter-tops can be coupled with a moulded, integral sink for a sleek, sculpted look, sink colour can either match the counter-top exactly or complement it. Edge banding and either border options are also there.

BRASS AND COPPER SINKS

These strikingly elegant surface are outstanding as accents. Since these sinks are very difficult to maintain, they are used for style, or at places where it is used occasionally.

COMPOSITE QUARTZ

This material is a mixture of quartz and acrylic. Composite quartz kitchen sinks are tough and durable. They are scratch-resistant and are not affected by alkalis, and acid used in the kitchen. Available in many colours, these sinks are nonporous and hence stain proof. These are available in many colours and configurations-one bowl, one and a half bowl and two bowls with or without drain boards.

KITCHEN FAUCETS

Kitchen faucets such as taps, stopcocks, etc. are used to regulate the supply of water. These faucets are available in the market in various materials like chromium plated metal, brass, power coated metal, aluminium or synthetic metal (symet). These faucets are available in various shapes, sizes and designs to suit various needs.

Taps can either be well mounted or fixed on horizontal surface such as rim of the sink. Wall mounted taps leave the rim clear and are easier to clean. Kitchen sink taps are like any other bathroom tap except for the difference that the spout of the sink is long so that the big utensils can easily be washed without any obstruction (to get a clear place between the sides of the sink and the utensils). All taps should operate smoothly the throughout their opening and closing range and tap handles should be convenient to use.

The taps with handles have either half-turn, quarter-turn or full-turn operation. Single level tap is much convenient to use as it is operated by simply changing the direction of lever. There are special kinds of taps too, the kitchen taps are available with aerators to avoid the splash of water. The aerator filters the water and mixes air bubbles with it. So that one does not get splash.

As mentioned earlier, there are basically two types of taps: one with vertical inlet is known as pillar cock and the other with horizontal inlet is called bib cock.

Following are the basic types of faucets available in the market.

Pillar cocks

Pillar cocks are the taps with vertical inlet which can be fixed on the horizontal surface, i.e. rim of the sink.

Bib Cocks

Bib cocks are taps with horizontal intels and are mounted on the wall.

Stop Cocks

Stop cocks are used to control the flow of water entering the taps. Stop cocks are fitted below the sink and are also used to regulate the quantity of hot and cold water in the mixer (Fig. 3.4)

Mixer Taps

Mainly there are two types of water supply to the kitchen sinks- cold and hot water. One 'option' is to have two separate taps for them and mix them in the utensil to achieve the desired temperature. This has become old fashioned now.

The most convenient one is to use mixer tap which mixes hot and cold water in the tap itself and one gets water at the desired temperature. Mixer taps are either operated by knobs or a single lever. For the first type of mixer tap, two separate stop cocks are provided. One each for hot and cold water supply. The flow and temperature of water through tap can be achieved by regulating the amount of hot or cold water as desired with the help of two separate cocks. Single lever operation is much easier and convenient to use. The flow and mixing of hot and cold water can be regulated by just changing the direction of a single lever which is easy to operate. Mixer taps are either wall mixers or rim mixers.

Wall mixers

Wall mixers are the mixer taps which are mounted on the walls. Wall mixers are either operated by a single lever or two knobs-one each for hot and cold water.

Rim mixer

These mixers are fixed on the horizontal surface, either on the rim of the sink or counter surface. Rim mixers are also operated either by different hot and cold water knobs or a single lever. They are available in various shapes and designs.

KITCHEN EQUIPMENT

Market is full of latest labour – and time – saving machines, positioning equipment of efficient use is only half the equation. Fundamental decisions must also be made on the range function one requires, their merits and demerits, if the wrong choice is made, it is not only wasting time and money, but losing valuable kitchen space as well that could be put to better use. Here is the survey of kitchen equipment and appliances that are available in the market.

Cook Tops

There are many types of cook taps available in the market, depending on the type of energy used-gas units and electric units. Gas units heat and cool quickly and the flame is visible and easy to control. Electric units provide low, even heat, Unless down venting model is used, the cook tap will require an overhead ventilation system, typically, cook tops have two or four burners, though some models have more.

Conventional Gas Cook Tops

A conventional gas cook top has two burners—one small and one large with a side connection—a rubber pipe leading to the liquefied petroleum gas (LPG) cylinder underneath the counter. These stoves are easy to clean. These cook tops are available in four burners, too. Commonly used cook tops is of stainless steel or nickel chrome finish.

There cook tops are also available with grilling as well as auto ignition option as well, single burner as well as three burners options are also there. The gas burner with a hot plate or electric coil combination is also available.

Electric coil and hot plate

Electric coil stoves are also available with one, two or four coil options, normally available vitreous enabled body to prevent against, corrosion and the body is cool even when the coil is hot. Heating coils heat up very fast and cool off slowly.

Cooking range

Ranges combine cook top and oven in a single unit, model choices and finishes are as varied as those offered in separate units. Available in all gas, gas/electric, auto ignition, motorised, rotisserie models, a few are available with cylinder compartment as well. Most popular are the gas cum electrically operated in which three gas burners and one electric hot plate or coil, separate grill and oven chamber are there. There burners, grill operates on gas and oven on electricity.

The energy consumption in various kinds of cook tops are:

a) In case four gas burners - Gas consumption of two burner is 185 gram/hr at 30 g/cm^2 and another two burner is 155 g/hr at 30 g/cm^2 and that of grill is 234 g/hr at Gmf/cm the total capacity of a gas cylinder is 14 kg.

b) Electric oven – 2300 W.

c) In case of cooking range has all gas options. From burners – two burners at 185 g/hr and two at 155 g/hr; grill at 234 g/hr; oven at 295 gram/hr.

d) In case three gas and one electric hot plate option; Three gas burners – two at 189 g/hr and one at 143 g/hr.

REFRIGERATORS AND FREEZERS

Fridge

Freezers come in several configurations side by side; with the freezer on top or the freezer below.

Refrigerators are available in 60-690 litre capacity. The efficiency of the refrigerator depends on the internal space allocation. There are single - door, two-door, three-and four door refrigerator with two or three compartments - one freezer one chilling compartment and one main storage area.

A Frost free unit, in which air is changed continuously, means there is no build up of ice. No- frost models automatically defrost the fridge and freezer and adjust humidity.

Energy factor

Refrigerators and freezers are basically insulated containers. A compressor, consisting of an electric motor which drives a pump, circulate gases which attract heat and dissipate warm air out of the fridge and freezer. The gases act as coolant.

Deep freezers

Deep freezers are available in two types. Top opening horizontal type deep freezers and front opening upright deep freezers.

Top opening chest freezers, are usually less expensive than upright models, and are often more economical to operate. Because cold air sinks, chest freezers do not lose as much cooled air when they're opened as upright do. Most chest freezers require manual defrosting, but with less frequency than manual defrost upright model.

Upright freezers comes in both frost free and manual defrost models. Shelves in upright freezers make them more convenient for organizing the frozen food; there's no digging or heavy lifting when one needs to use the freezer. Upright freezers also occupy less floor space, 110 to 308/463.

Both chest and upright models are available with some or all of these popular options.

A 'power' on light on the freezer cabinet quickly indicates whether on not the unit is working, if a freezer malfunctions or is accidentally turned off, it may spoil the stored food.

Organizers such as baskets and juice can racks are available for upright models to maximize storage space and easy food and beverage retrieval.

Dishwashers

Dishwashers are normally installed near the sink, they are either portable or are installed within the cabinet. An electric switch for the dishwater is needed near the sink, but away from the water tap.

Most of the dishwashers load from the front. The following points need to be kept in mind when ordering a dishwasher.

1. **Capacity**–Choose a model that's big enough for a day's worth of your family's daily dishes.
2. **Strainer/filtering system**–Strainer plates at the bottom of unit keep bits of food from dogging the drain. In some models, a self- cleansing filter removes tiny particles of food during the wash cycle; a back wash system that cleans the filter and flushes food down the drain.
3. **Soft food disposal**–This option liquefies soft foods for disposal into waste water; you do not need to prerinse dirty dishes in the sink.

4. **Detergent` and rinse additive dispenser**—These dispensers automatically release detergent and rinse additives at the proper times.
5. **Preheating cycles**—Some dishwashers have a preheater that saves energy by letting you operate your water heater at a lower temperature.

Additional features on portable models include faucet connectors that let you use running water while the dishwasher is operating.

A regular cycle cleans normally solid dishes.

A quick cycle provides a short wash for lightly solid dishes. A gentle (or china/crystal) cycle aerates the water or softness its force.

A heavy duty cycle extends the normal cycle or adds an extra wash cycle for tough jobs.

A soak/scrub (or pots and pans) cycle briefly wets the dishes, then a soaking solution softens the food before the regular wash.

A power saver cycle conserves energy by letting dishes air dry rather than using the heating element sometimes, the power saver cycle also by passes the beat booster that maintains a minimum water temperature during washing

A sanitizing cycle heats water to a factory set temperature to sanitise dishes.

A rinse and hold cycle rinses dishes in short, no detergent cycle.

This prevents food from souring and drying dishes while a full dishwasher load accumulates.

A dish warmer cycle lets you take advantage of the drying stages of the regular cycle to prevent dishes for serving hot foods at meal time.

Stainless steel interiors are more durable and less likely to take on odours or stain then enamel. Copper, silver and aluminium items discolour when they washed in steel due to a reaction between the metals.

Normally the unit is equipped with a dish basket offering many washing possibilities according to the shape and size of the cooking utensils and dinner sets. The model with automatic opening of the door at the end of the programme is the best, which allows faster drying of the dishes.

In India available dishwasher is 56 × 45 × 52.5 cm with a capacity which can hold complete dinner set of six members.

Waste disposers

A garbage disposer cuts, shreds and grinds food wastes and simply flushes them down the drain. It saves a lot of trouble of cleaning up after the cooking. Food scraps go right into the sink, instead of the dustbin. These disposers are available with sink connection. Disposers are connected under the sink.

The use of waste disposers is very easy. Just drop the food scraps down the drain and with the disposer on. The disposer liquefies and flushes food waste into the drain. Messy kitchen scraps, when left in the dustbin, can attract insects and create an unpleasant odour.

The food disposers can grind vegetables, fish, egg shells, rinds and cores, fish bones, meat leftovers, bones, peels, etc. the dustbin will mostly contain dry waste.

Trash compactor

A trash compactor reduces the size of the trash to a fraction of the normal size. A family of four can compress a week's accumulated trash (including bottles, cartons, papers, plastics and other dry food waste) into one bag full or bucket full. These compactors need special disposal bags.

Microwaves

Microwaves are not really 'ovens' at all. High frequency radio waves penetrate deep into the food, vibrating water molecules so they generate heat. This heat is what cooks the food.

Power, performance and capacity vary according to the manufacturer and model. Some models have electronic sensing systems which determine how much and how long raw food needs to be cooked. Reliance on a microwave is for heating snacks, a good spot is near the refrigerator. If it is a cooking utensil, it might be used to create a second cook area much the way a second sink creates and additional food preparation centre. Microwaves can perch on work-tops, be treated as a small appliance, or be built into base or wall cupboards or inset into splash backs though remember to provide for proper ventilation.

Food cooks quickly with high frequency microwaves but they seldom brown. Some models offer a separate browning element.

Oven, toaster and griller (OTG)

An OTG perform all the three functions, i.e. as an oven, toaster and griller. It has two heating elements- one on top and another at the bottom, which can be controlled by the switches on the panel. One can select upper heating mode or lower heating mode depending on the type of cooking. These are available in models with 15 to 30 litre capacity.

These ovens are available with heat blast control for good cooking, which circulates hot air around the oven cavity. These are more energy efficient than radiant ovens, cut cooking time by 30 percent operating at reduced temperature.

Following are some functions available in all or some of the OTGs:

(i) Thermostat control- separate temperature controls for different types of cooking.

(ii) Timer - Sets the time along with other controls.

(iii) Enameled top which can let it be used for cooking as well.

(iv) Motorized rotisserie, automatic or manual, with barbe-cues skewers.

(v) Multi-level wire grill rack.

(vi) Vitreous enameled backing tray.

(vii) Long heating elements for uniform heat distribution.

(viii) Illuminated interiors to assess the progress of the food.

Washing machines; washing machines are either semiautomatic or fully automatic. A semiautomatic comes with twin- tubs, one for washing/rinsing and other for spin drying, thus occupying a lot of storage space. Water is to be filled manually or by an inbuilt devise, which controls flow from a domestic line to where the washing machine is connected. It has to be stopped manually to avoid overflow. Subsequent to the adding of soap powder, the timer has to be set to carry out washing operation. Clothes are transferred manually from the washing tub to the spinning tub. A corner space with drain facility is all that is required for this machine. It is medium priced, needs more floor space and has 3-5 kg capacity.

On the other hand, a fully automatic washing machine has a single tub. All operations-washing, rinsing and drying-are done by a preset timing device. Domestic water pipeline with a minimum water pressure is required. It does not need any supervision. The washing is totally automatic and gives an indication as soon as washing operation is complete.

A washing operation is carried out by using one of the three systems—pulsating, agitating or tumbling.

1. **Pulsating system**—a pulsator (impeller) is mounted inside the tub in a horizontal or angular position at the bottom. The pulsator rotated by the motor creates turbulence, the nature, quality and speed of which depend on size, design location and speed of pulsator as well as design of wash tub. This system is used both in semiautomatic and automatic washing machines with top loading facility.

2. **Agitator system**—Agitating strokes are created by a centrally located vertical shaft with built in flexible fins (blades or vanes). The number of oscillating strokes per minute, size and design of the agitator are the main criteria for its end result. This system is used by and large in fully automatic machines. Noise level is high as compared to other systems. The of oscillating strokes per minute (about 65) is considered less as compared to the speed of pulsator per minute (about 700). This system is preferred for its slow speed due to which clothes suffer less damage. This is again used in top loading machines.
3. **Tumbling system**—Clothes are tumbled down in a perforated and horizontally mounted rotating drum. Projections inside the drum moves them upward and drops them down. This system is used in fully automatic and front loading machines with built - in drain pump to let out the water after the operation. The other choice is either a top loading or front loading or front loading machine, front loader uses water more efficiently, but are more expensive and do not hold as big a load. In front loading, clothes are difficult to remove in case of a power failure in the middle of an operations water spills from the tub. Power consumption is also high as it uses a heater to warm water.

The capacity of washing machines is another very essential point, machine capacity is indicated by the weight of the clothes it can wash in one load. In case of twin tubs, load pattern is different for wash and spin dry. Capacity generally varies between 3 and 6 kg.

The capacity should be decided based on the weight of the clothes expected to be washed daily or alternately for the family. Normally a capacity of 4 kg in deal for a family of 4 to 6 members.

KITCHEN STANDARDS

Before giving final shape to the kitchen planning, it is necessary to know various standard dimensions which are rooted to the kitchen activities. The standard dimensions are based on the space needed for various human activities. The anthropometric related to the kitchens.

Five work centres

The real key to planning a good, desirable and efficient kitchen layout is to concentrate on the five work centres, allowing for both adequate counter top space and storage in each area.

Refrigerator and food storage centre

A minimum of 400 mm, or desirable 600 mm of counter-top space is required on the handle side of the refrigerator as a landing area for groceries. Ideally, the refrigerator is at the end of the cabinet run, near the access door. The clear space in front of the refrigerator should not be less than 70 cm. Depth of the counter should be 60 cm.

Sink and cleanup centre

Sink is either single, double or triple bowl or without drain board. Figure a minimum of 600 mm of counter space on one side of the sink and 900 mm on the other side. In case another smaller sink is provided, these clearances can be smaller.

Room for movement in front of sink should not be less than 80 cm. Free space in front of dishwasher is 100 cm for opening.

Range and cooking centre

At least 400 mm (desirable 600 mm) of counter top area on each side of the range or cook top as a landing area for hotpots and casseroles, and to allow pot handles to be turned to the sides while pots are in use. The same is applicable in case of top on island and peninsula. Minimum free space in front of top to bend and use the lower shelf should be 100 mm.

Food preparation and chopping centre

This auxiliary centre is ideally located between the refrigerator and the sink; a minimum of 1,050 mm of counter top and maximum of 2,100 mm is required. Different type of work require different counter top height.

Serving centre

This optional work centre is located between the range and sink, size of this centre is between 900 mm and 2,100 mm, this space can be shared with both cleanup and cooking centres. Free space in front of the counter should be minimum 50 cm, if hands are free and 80 cm when carrying a tray, etc. Depth of the work surface should be 45 cm.

Standard dimensions

The standard minimum clearances in a well planned kitchen. These dimensions ensure enough space for the cook; enough door clearances for free access to cabinets, dishwasher and refrigerator and enough traffic lanes for diners to comfortably enter and exit breakfast noon.

Vertical dimensions are equally important to a kitchen in good working order. Design cupboards, shelves and drawers to minimise bending down and stretching. Bending down is more tiresome and you need more space to do it. Following are the standard depths and heights for base and wall cabinets and shelves, plus recommended heights for stools and eating counters.

It is not necessary to plan a kitchen with all the work tops at one uniform height. Delicate complex such as mixing, chopping need a higher surface. Heavier tasks like kneading flour, etc. require the use of an upper arm and strain back muscles so the work top should ideally be correspondingly lower. The cook top can be lowered to the height from where you can see into the pans during cooking.

While it is good to have a tailored work top suited to the user for performing specific tasks, work taps that vary too much in height can create jarring disharmony and can overly complicate small kitchens.

Changes in work top level, unless treated with due common sense, can make a kitchen a more hazardous place than necessary. A change in level should be avoided where it interrupts a useful flow of continuous work surface.

Where work tops of different heights are used on adjacent walls, the higher counter should continue into the corner rather than the lower one.

2

Modern Developments in Kitchen Equipment

MICROWAVE OVEN

The microwave oven which is a relatively modern cooking appliance, can be described as an electronic cooking device in which food is heated by means of high frequency radio waves, known as microwaves. The microwaves are produced by a power source identified as a magnetron. This form of cooking was developed in the U.S.A. as a peaceful application of the principles used in radar during World War II.

The conventional methods of cookery employ the use of conducted, convected and radiated heat. As can be seen these methods provide heat which penetrated food gradually from the exterior of the centre. Microwaves on the other hand do not give such heat to food, nor do they control heat within the oven cavity as experienced with conventional methods. Instead the oven is designed to beam high-frequency energy from the magnetron at the food so molecules of water in food are violently disturbed creating molecular friction. The friction generates heat, which converts the food's moisture into steam, heating the food throughout. Furthermore, microwaves have the capacity to penetrate through certain foods instantly and produce heat wherever moisture is present. However the sealing and colouring effects associated with conventional methods are not noticeably achieved. The depth of wave penetration will depend, amongst other factors, upon the food's density but generally waves extend into food from between 2 and 3 inches and beyond this depth the passage of heat relies on conduction only.

Characteristics of microwaves

Microwaves like light rays have the following important characteristics:

(a) penetration;

(b) reflection;

(c) absorption.

Penetration

The waves are able to pass through certain substances without being absorbed. For example, glass, plastics, chinaware, scarcely absorb microwaves and allow them to pass through. Therefore food containers made form such materials do not become hot from the microwaves but they may conduct heat from the food being cooked in the oven cavity.

Reflection

Microwaves are reflected from such substances as metals, i.e. good conductors of electricity. This characteristic is used to advantage within the oven in that waves are reflected from the metallic surfaces. Consequently foods places in the oven absorb the waves from all directions, the cooking period is fast and the need to turn foods for even cooking is eliminated. However, as a result of this reflecting characteristic, metal or metal-banded containers are generally unsuitable for use in microwave ovens, as waves are reflected from the container surfaces and not absorbed by the food.

Absorption

Cooking is achieved by the molecular disturbance created when the radio wave energy is absorbed by the food. As previously noted substances containing a high proportion of water easily absorb microwaves and this is true not only of food but of paper or cloth soaked with water.

Construction

A microwave oven consists of the following main components:

1. *Power transformer*—supplies power to the magnetron;
2. *Magnetron*—produces high frequency electro-magnetic waves (microwaves);
3. *Waveguide*—guides the microwaves form the magnetron into the oven cavity;
4. *Oven cavity*—a metal box in which food is placed for cooking by microwaves which enter from above;
5. *Finder/window*—a window in the oven door containing very fine perforations dimensioned to prevent any loss of microwaves energy and to enable viewing of food without opening the oven door;
6. S*tirrer fan/agitator*—used to distribute the microwaves coming into the oven from the waveguide and to diffuse reflected energy to achieve more even cooking;
7. *Stirrer motor*—drives the stirrer fan;
8. *Oven shelf*—shelf upon which containers and food are placed for cooking.

Ovens are fitted with a built-in ventilation system to effect cooling of the magnetron and other vital components. The air may be drawn through a special dust filter that keeps the electrical and mechanical parts dust-free. Other refinements include timer controls for defrosting, cooking and reheating with automatic signaling devices. The controls may also incorporate a 'repeating feature', which enables the operator to cook a number of similar items one after the other, without having to re-set the timer. All ovens feature automatic safety devices that inactivate microwave power when the oven door is opened.

Various designs and sizes of oven are manufactured. Size is measured by output power, e.g. 1 kW, 2 kW, etc., and not by the size of the oven cavity, oven dimensions are chosen on the basis of the frequency used and the optimum exploitation of generated energy.

Technologists are continually improving equipment and microwave ovens are no exception. Three problems commonly associated with microwave cookery are as follows:

(a) uneven cooking or heating due to 'cold spots' (uneven wave distribution and absorption) in the oven;
(b) inability of microwave energy to achieve significant colour changes (browning) of food compared with conventional cooking methods;
(c) relatively small oven capacity, which places a limit on its utility in some catering situations, e.g. volume catering.

To counteract these problems certain innovations and technological advances have been implemented.

Counteracting cold spots

(a) Dual magnetrons—in order to overcome 'cold spots' manufacturers have fitted some ovens with two magnetrons, which produce more microwave energy for distribution within the oven.

(b) Turntable—other manufacturers have incorporated the revolving oven shelf (turn-table) to ensure that foods do not experience damage throughout the length of the cooking period.

Colouring Foods (browning)

(a) Techniques to effect browning of food include the development of combined units that incorporate a microwave oven with a separate infra-red grill, where the grill is used to colour the food prior to or following the period of cooking by microwaves.

(b) **Micro-browners** – another patented development is the use of micro-browners, which comprise specially designed ceramic containers that are able to absorb microwave energy. The containers are pre-heated in the microwave oven and their surface becomes sufficiently heated to give colour to foods placed on then, as would be expected by cooking on a griddle or in a shallow frying vessel. The use of these ceramic containers involves the turning of foods when colouring of both sides is required.

Micro-air ovens

Micro-air ovens may be described as being different from but related to the conventional microwave oven. They differ in the following ways:

(a) they combine forced-air convection and microwave energy in a single unit;

(b) they offer increased oven capacity and can be used to carry out most of the culinary operations associated with conventional and microwave cookery;

(c) they effect the browning of foods generally associated with conventional cooking methods;

(d) the oven cavity becomes heated during the cooking period;

(e) when combined systems are operated the cooking times are longer than with microwaves but are shorter when compared with conventional cooking times;

(f) both cooking methods can be used simultaneously or independently as required;

(g) traditional containers can be successfully used in the oven including those made from metals.

Combined methods

The combined cooking is affected by the use of 'pulsed' microwaves (i.e. microwave energy is emitted intermittently at 7 second intervals throughout cooking), along with forced-air convected heat. Manufacturers claim that the oven will carry out most of the culinary operations associated with conventional and microwave units. The oven is most versatile in that it combines the speed of microwaves with the fast heat transfer of forced-air convection to cook with traditional colour, texture and flavour associated with high quality foods.

Oven capacity

With a large potential capacity and throughput the use of the micro-wave oven is extended over a wide range of catering operations. For example, when used as the combined system it is able to cope with a 1×1 Gastronorm tray or six to eight separate items at the same time. Alternatively when used independently as a convection oven the insertion of a three tier rack allows for the cooking of greater numbers of portions e.g., multiportion packs (50 to 80 portions) reheated at the same time.

Examples of cooking times

Recent examples quoted by manufacturers include:

(a) 12 kg turkey in 55 minutes;

(b) 7 kg of pork in 48 minutes.

GENERAL FACTORS ON MICROWAVE COOKING

The speed at which food is electronically heated is determined by a number of variables and the following general observations may be of value.

Chemical structure

Food scientists state that in general the more complex the chemical structure of food the more quickly the product will attain a high temperature. For example, one litre of milk will reach boiling point before one litre of water.

Shape and form

Thinner pieces of food cook more quickly than larger portions as it is more difficult for microwaves to penetrate to the core of large, thick pieces. So cutting and slicing food into smaller/thinner portions enables the microwaves to penetrate more quickly and often instantaneously throughout the product, speeding up the heating process.

Arranging foods

For even cooking or heating food should be distributed evenly in containers. Piling foods on to a tray in an ad hoc fashion may result in uneven cooking or heating.

Loss of moisture

Food tends to release water when heated by microwaves. In order to minimize loss of moisture foods may be placed in a covered container or wrapped in plastic film.

Quantities of food

When cooking a small quantity of food any microwave energy not absorbed by that item is wasted. This wasted energy could have been used to cook a larger quantity over a similar cooking period. In general an increase in the volume of food required a further increase in cooking time. However if full use is made of available energy cooking times remain short and do not necessarily increase proportionately with the volume of food.

Initial temperature of foods

The lower the initial temperature of food before cooking or heating commences the longer the time required to complete the operation, when heating frozen items either to thaw or cook the speed of wave penetration is retarded because ice-crystals act as wave reflectors and the rise in temperature is slowed down.

State of the food

Microwaves are able to deal with food in a raw, partly cooked or completely cooked state. The heating times will vary accordingly.

Food containers

The materials chosen for use as containers are those that are little of the high frequency energy. They must be capable of withstanding high temperatures which are reached within the food during cooking, e.g. 100°C plus. The materials used must not reflect the microwaves (as is the case with metals) but allow them to pass through as light rays through a window. Cling-film wrap and roast-a-bags may be used as containers.

SUMMARY AND SAFETY

For recommended cooking/heating times and further detailed information consult recognized manufacturers.

It is believed that defective doors are the main source of radiation leakage from microwave ovens. Therefore, units are fitted with safety features to prevent leakage during cooking and also ensure that when the door seal is interrupted the oven will not function. However microwave ovens should be carefully checked against leakage or the possibility of exposure which could lead to microwave injury.

FORCED-AIR CONVECTION OVENS

A wide range of forced-air convection ovens are manufactured, designed to meet the specific needs of a variety of catering operations. These ovens may differ in their design specifications, energy source, output potentials, and utility in a similar way to conventional ovens. The principal difference between a convection oven and an ordinary (conventional) oven is the accelerated air movement within the oven cavity and the varying heat inputs applied.

According to a leading designer in this area, forced-air convection ovens may, for the sake of simplicity, be categorized as follows:

Hard units

These are ovens that have the highest air movement speed, generally combined with the highest heat input. These units are most suitable for the reheating of bulk and individual frozen foods, but are not suitable for prime cooking or baking.

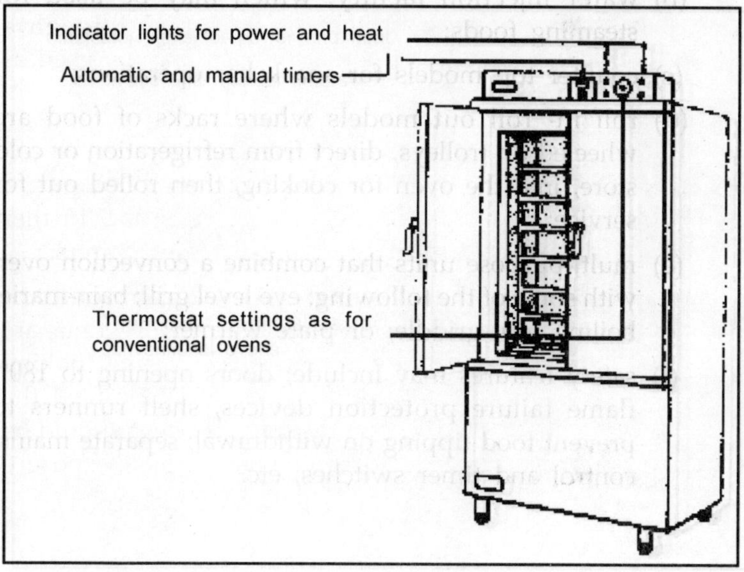

Medium units

These are ovens that have a lower air movement speed, generally combined with a lower heat input. These ovens are suitable for prime cooking, some baking and if required reheating frozen foods.

Soft units

These are ovens that have the lowest air movement speed and heat input, these ovens are suitable for some prime cooking and for baking but unsatisfactory for reheating frozen food because the time taken to reheat may constitute a health hazard.

Therefore when purchasing forced-air convection ovens, prospective buyers should consult recognized specialist who can advise on the best selection to suit the buyer's specific requirements. Some special design features which illustrate this point are listed below:

(a) bakery convection oven with steam injection facility;

(b) water injection facility, which may be used for steaming foods;

(c) counter top models for snack bar operations;

(d) roll in- roll out models where racks of food are wheeled on trolleys, direct from refrigeration or cold store, into the oven for cooking, then rolled out for service;

(e) multi-purpose units that combine a convection oven with some of the following: eye level grill; bain-marie; boiling top; griddle; or plate warmer;

(f) safety features may include; doors opening to 180°; flame failure protection devices, shelf runners to prevent food tipping on withdrawal; separate mains, control and timer switches; etc.

The principle of forced-air convection

On heating, air rises and when trapped within an oven cavity forms a convection current, which circulates within the oven. In ordinary ovens the current of heated air circulated slowly, which affects the time taken to reach the required cooking temperature. In addition variations of temperature, within the oven, occur particularly following the introduction of cooler air once the oven doors are opened.

In contrast, when employing a forced-air convection oven the circulating current of hot air is forced speedily around the oven chamber by a motorized fan or blower. This technique creates a more even and constant temperature throughout the oven because of improved heat distribution, and also shortens the time taken to pre-heat the oven. Furthermore the current of continuous moving air strips away the thin layer of moisture and cool air from the surface of food placed into the oven, allowing heat to penetrate and cook more quickly.

When using the convection oven cooking temperatures are lower and cooking times shorter because heat is used more efficiently. As a result of the improved distribution of heat, foods may be cooked successfully in any part of the oven eliminating the need to open the doors and move food from one shelf to another, it should be noted that not all the food in the oven will be cooked to exactly the same degree but the variations experienced are acceptable.

Advantages

Manufacturers claim that when using forced-air convection ovens in correct circumstances and following adequate training certain advantages accrue:

(a) time saving - cooking and labour time;

(b) energy saving - reduction in cooking temperatures, cooking times and pre-heating times;

(c) space utilization - ovens are designed to make maximum use of production space and at the same time increase volume output;

(d) product quality and yield-foods cook more evenly giving a high quality finish with less shrinkage and therefore a higher portion yield. This is due to the shorter cooking time at lower temperatures.

Examples taken from a convection oven cooking guide

Food	Mark	Min	Shelves (Oven capacity)
Sirloin of beef 3 kg (6 lb) joints	5	115	4
Pork joints 1 kg (2½ lb)	6	55	4
Baked potatoes	7	45-60	6
Vol-au-vents	8	10	6
Rice pudding	1	60	6

Pressure steamers

General features

Modern pressure steamers vary in design, size, versatility, efficiency and volume output potential. Consequently models are designed to meet the needs of different types of catering operation. These models range from small back bar units designed to effect fast cooking and reheating of foods, to larger models designed to cope quickly and effectively with volume catering. Certain models feature more than one cooking compartment, providing the caterer with operational versatility so that large and small amounts of food can be steamed independently or simultaneously as demanded by the customer.

Steamer trays/pans are identified as solid/plain or perforated with either one being selected for use as required by the culinary operation in hand. As a general guide solid/

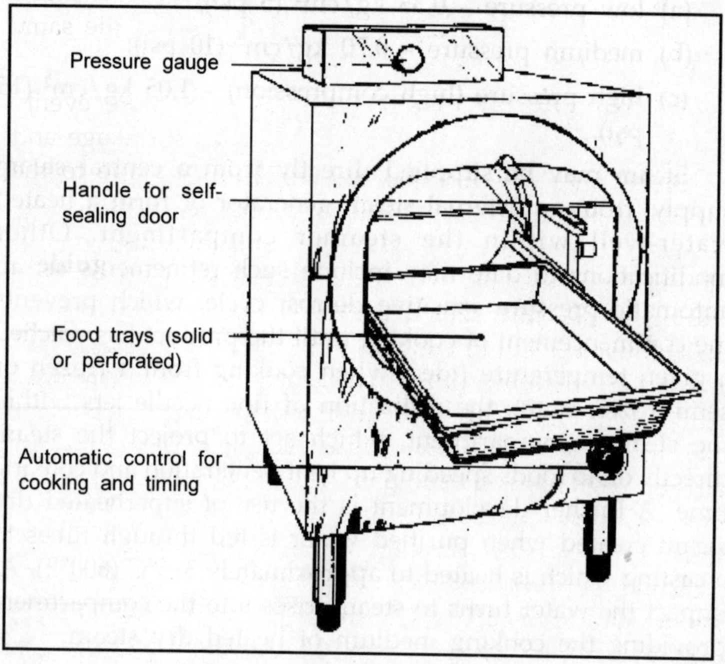

plain trays are used where an amount of liquid is needed within the tray to assist cooking, or where the juice of the food being steamed is to be retained of culinary purposes, e.g. chicken essence for a sauce. Perforated trays, however, are employed when no liquid is required to assist in the cooking process, and also when foods are to be well drained. Manufacturers provide detailed charts concerning the steaming of various foods but the experienced chef will soon recognize the culinary potential of the modern pressure steamers.

Steam supply and pressure

All pressure steamers cook foods by using the concentrated heat of steam at varying pressures. The pressures used generally range from 0.35-1.05 kg/cm^2 (5-15 psi) and are often described as:

(a) low pressure - 0.35 kg/cm^2 (5 psi);

(b) medium pressure - 0.70 kg/cm^2 (10 psi);

(c) high pressure (high compression) - 1.05 kg/cm^2 (15 psi).

Steam may be supplied directly from a central steam supply, from an external steam generator or form a heated water-well within the steamer compartment. Other modifications to date may include such refinements as: an automatic pressure sensitive defrost cycle, which prevents the commencement of cooking until the product has reached a given temperature (ideal when cooking from a frozen or semi-frozen state); the utilization of fine needle jets within the steamer compartment, which act to project the steam directly on to foods speeding up heat penetration and cooking time. A further development is the use of superheated dry steam created when purified water is fed through tubes to a casting which is heated to approximately 315°C (600°F). At impact the water turns to steam, rises into the compartment providing the cooking medium of heated dry steam.

FOODS AND COOKING TIMES

A wide variety of raw or pre-cooked foods may be steamed to effect cooking or reheating. Steamers according to manufacturers' specifications are able to cope effectively with many foods from a thawed or frozen condition. Cooking times commence once the correct steam pressure is reached and most models make the use of automatic timers to control the selected cooking period.

When using high compression steamers recommended cooking times for listed products are remarkably swift, with the foods being cooked in an environment of dry steam from which air has been expelled. Manufacturers claim that this form of steaming prevents oxidation of vitamins and mineral salts, assists in retaining the natural colour, flavour, aroma and texture of foods during cooking, certain products however are preferably steamed at low to medium pressure to achieve best results, e.g. steamed savoury or sweet puddings, and caterers may experiment with the use of pressure and cooking times to identify their culinary requirements, it must be stated that as the weight/load of food being steamed increases so in general does the cooking time but these increases do not appear to be extensive (see the table below).

Examples of recommended cooking times (approx) using a high compression steamer at 1.05 kg/cm² (15 psi)

Product	Load in kg (lb)	Timer setting (min)
Brussel sprouts (fresh)	2 (5)	4-6
Brussel sprouts (frozen)	6 (15)	11-13
Fish steaks (thawed)	1 (2)	3-6
Lobster, 1 kg (2½ lb) each (thawed)	6 (15)	11-12
Whole chickens, 1.5 kg (3 lb) each (thawed)	9 (18)	30

Innovations in culinary practices enable many traditional dishes to be cooked in the steamer. For example foods that require the colouring and sealing associated with shallow frying or braising may be sealed and coloured in the traditional manner before being placed into the steamer to complete cooking, fish portions may be steamed rather than poached and the masking/accompanying sauce prepared independently (an ideal technique for large scale banqueting).

Safety factors

When using high compression steamers the door cannot be opened until all the pressure within the compartment has been released. When the steam is released from a conventional steamer it is wise to use the steamer door as a protective shield to safeguard oneself form hot steam that may remain within the compartment following initial steam release.

Summary

The information provided is in broad, general terms. Detailed technical information is available from manufacturers who specialize in the production and marketing of such equipment, the purchaser therefore is well advised to make full use of the advice concerning the many options now available.

PRESSURELESS CONVECTION STEAMER

Manufacturers of this most recent development in steaming equipment have designed a pressureless steaming unit, which equates with the efficiency and culinary utility of the modern high compression steamers previously described, it is argued that ideally food is best cooked at the lowest effective cooking temperature in order to avoid cellular damage, excess nutritional

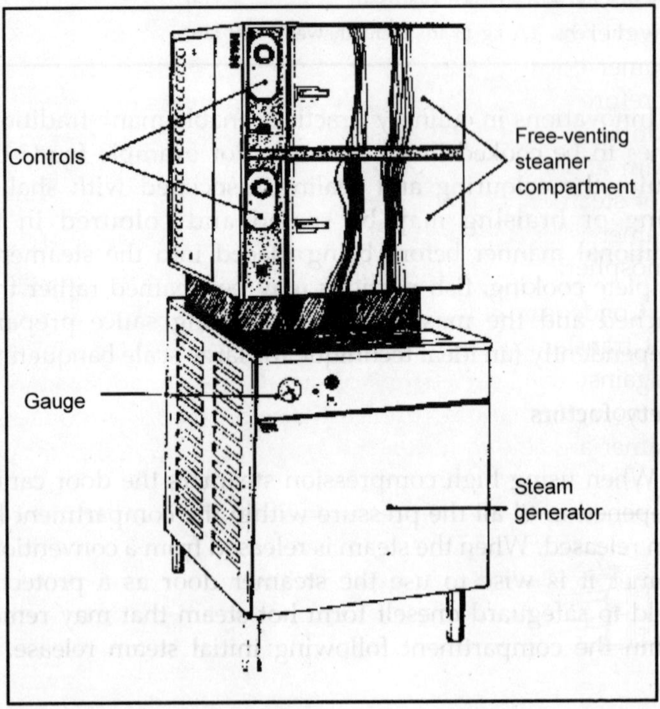

loss, over shrinkage and product discoloration, furthermore cooking by steam in a constantly venting compartment (pressureless compartment) eliminates gases, volatiles and other undesirable by-products, which can have unfavourable effects upon the colour and flavour of foods. Therefore efficient cooking is ideal when using low temperature, constantly venting steam, but two major obstacles may remain:

(a) air;

(b) condensate.

Manufacturers state that the presence of only 0.5% of air in a steam environment can reduce the heat transfer coefficient by as much as 50%. Furthermore as air is an effective insulator its presence around food acts as a barrier to efficient heat transfer. A cooking compartment containing steam and air can only supply the temperature of the partial pressure of the steam and not of the total chamber pressure. It must however be stated that manufacturers of a high compression steamer claim to expel all air form the cooking atmosphere, therefore overcoming these problems, however physicists endorse that more heat is available for cooking in 1 lb of steam at atmospheric (zero pressure) than is available at 1 lb of steam at 15 lb of pressure, the pressureless convection steamer is designed to use the potential energy of steam at atmospheric pressure in an effective and efficient manner.

Condensate, it is claimed, is an additional barrier to efficient heat transfer because it forms around the food and insulates it against the heat energy of steam. By employing modern technology, manufacturers of the pressureless convection steamer are able to utilize the lowest practical temperature of

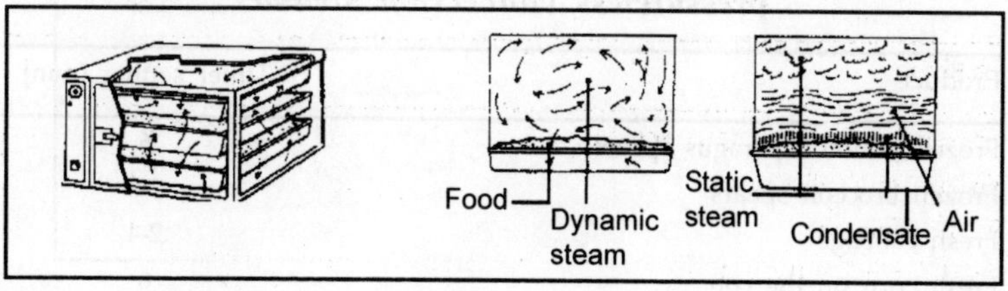

steam i.e. 100°C (212°F) at atmospheric (zero) pressure to cook foods efficiently and retain a high level of quality control. The purified steam is generated in a boiler under pressure before being introduced into the cooking compartment directly over the food within. Because the compartment is on a constantly free-venting system no pressure build up occurs (pressureless teaming). The steam is made to act like a piston forcing out the air. Turbulent, controlled forced convection steam strips away the layer of insulative condensate from foods and cooling steam and condensate from foods is continually replaced by a fresh supply of steam from the generator.

Coking therefore is achieved with low-temperature constantly-venting steam in a pressureless air-free environment of controlled convection, aptly described as cooking in a pressureless convection steamer. Certain models are for dual purpose and may also be used as pressure steamers. Other refinements may include automatic timers with each compartment independently controlled for versatility of use. Steamer or compartment doors seal automatically when closed and may be opened safely at any time because there is no pressure within.

Food cooked and trays used

As with high compression steamers a wide variety of foods can be cooked/reheated from raw/cooked states and from a thawed or frozen condition. Manufacturers provide guidelines concerning types of foods and cooking times involved. The types of steamer tray used are plain, solid or perforated and the same guidelines apply as for compression steamers.

Examples of approximate time settings recommended for pressureless convection steamer

Product	Timer setting (min)
Frozen jumbo asparagus spears	6
Frozen broccoli spears	2-3
Fresh cabbage	2-4
Fresh corn on the cob	6

Frozen corn on the cob	8-10
Frozen salmon steaks (200 g (8 oz) portions)	7
Frozen cod fillets	3
Fresh beef brisket (400 g (1 lb))	18-20

Summary

The information provided is of a general nature and interested caterers are advised to seek further and more detailed technical data from recognized sources.

LIQUIDIZER

The liquidizer is a piece of kitchen machinery which uses a high speed motor to drive specially designed stainless steel blades to chop, puree, or blend foods very quickly and efficiently, although it is not a large-scale piece of kitchen machinery its versatility and value are worth mentioning. This small machine operates at various speeds to suit the job in hand. It is particularly useful to the small volume caterer whose type of operation may not warrant investment in large-scale equipment to carry out similar work. Often the liquidizer

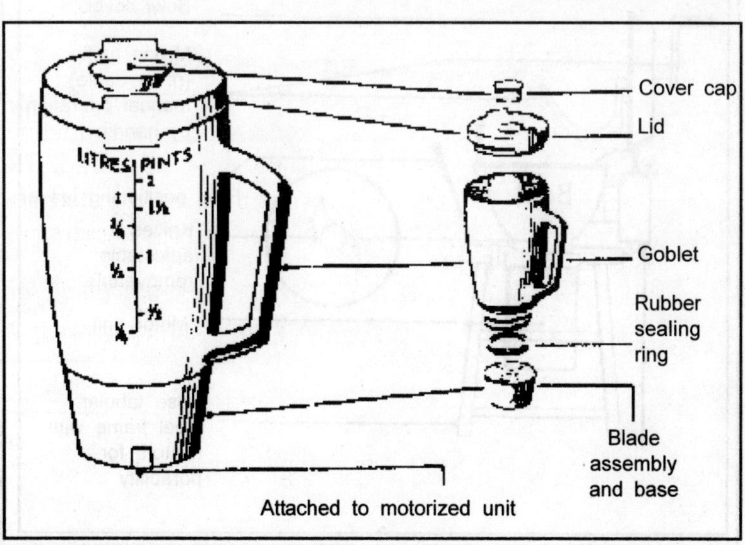

reduces labour intensity and time taken to complete certain tasks by eliminating traditional methods, which are often laborious, in addition it may improve the overall quality of a finished product, e.g. consistency and flavour of soups, sauces, fruit juices, fruit and vegetable purees and pates, etc.

Examples of culinary uses

According to manufacturers' recommendations, this machine may be used as follows:

(a) to puree or blend, soups, sauces, fruit juices and dressings;

(b) to puree various pates and fruit preparations;

(c) to crush ice cubes or nuts;

(d) to mix batters, etc.

VERTICAL CUTTER/MIXER (VCM)

The VCM is a relatively large piece of versatile kitchen machinery which is able to cut and mix ingredient simultaneously. The machine could be described as a type of large-scale liquidizer. The high speed motor drives any one of

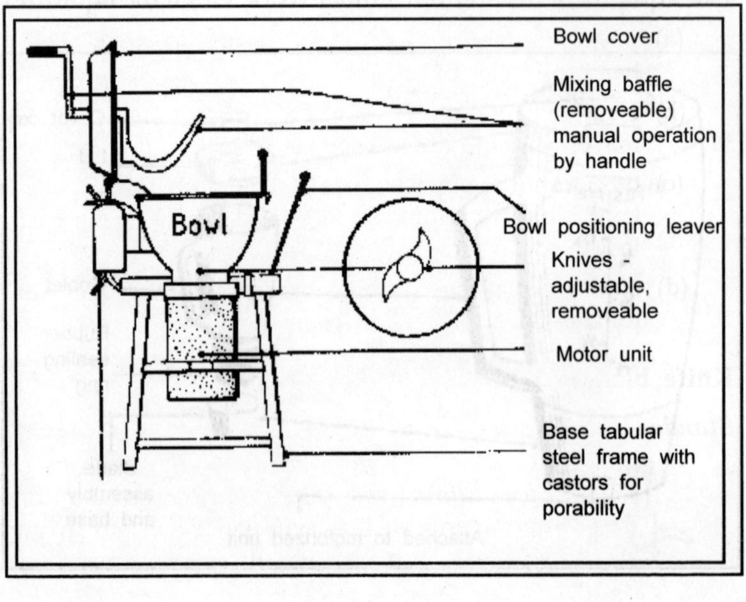

a variety of purpose designed, interchangeable stainless steel blades that are positioned inside the bowl according to the job in hand. This machine is ideally employed in situations that require a speedy preparation of large quantities of quality foods and bakery products. Manufacturers claim that speed, volume, increased product yield and quality are achieved as a result of the cutting action of the knife blades. The blades move at a high speed and slice the products whilst they are suspended in mid-air, without giving rise to bruising or mashing, where applicable it is also claimed that the natural juices and flavour of foods are retained. A full range of models of various capacities are available to carry out virtually any tasks that incorporate cutting, mixing or blending, machines are designed to suit both large and small operations but it is advisable to consult manufacturers for specialist information concerning the purchase of a VCM.

N.B. Certain models without tubular steel frame, may be clamped on to a suitable bench or table.

Examples of culinary uses

According to manufacturers' recommendations these machines may be used as follows:

(a) prepare quantities of raw foremeats, e.g. 12 kg (27 lb) hamburger mix in 40 sec;

(b) blend large volumes of soups and sauces in seconds, e.g. mayonnaise in 120 sec, soups in 30 sec;

(c) mix quantities of pastry and bread dough quickly, e.g. 11 kg (25 lb) bread dough in 90 sec, 11 kg (25 lb) pie pastry in 20 sec;

(d) cut/slice quantities of vegetables speedily, e.g. vegetables for coleslaw in 12 sec.

Knife blades

Standard accessories

Shaft with narrow knives is used for all cutting operations, such as sausage or hamburger mix, wieners, bologna and other meat products, vegetables for salads and coleslaw, pastry products, cake batters, cheese spreads, and making certain types of salad dressings and processing yeast doughs where a fine texture is desired.

Knead/mix shaft one-piece cast aluminium designed for mixing small quantities that require no cutting action.

Optional extras

Wide knives are used for the same applications as the narrow knives but are best suited for cutting frozen products (-2°C (28°F)) or in industrial applications where the products to be cut or mixed are very dense.

Narrow and wide wave cut knives are used for cutting oily products; nuts, corn mesa for Spanish foods, and some vegetables. Again, the wide knives are used for harder products.

Grating shaft is used for grating hard raw vegetables and for the mixing of dry ingredients.

Mixing shaft is used for blending and mixing large quantities of ingredients where not cutting action is required.

Cleaning

The machine may be cleaned using a 10 sec run with warm detergent water which is poured away and followed by hand wiping.

BRATT PAN

This piece of equipment derives its name form the German word 'Braten' translated refers to a number of cooking methods. Bratt pans are relatively new to the U.K. but have been widely and successfully used on the continent for many years, gas and electric models are manufactured and the cooking pan is mainly constructed of stainless steel or cast iron. Models vary in design, shape, potential utility with special features offered. The models are produced to meet various catering requirements, at present the models available are designed to meet the requirements of large volume catering but manufacturers hope to engineer a model to meet the needs of the smaller catering operation.

Special features may include:

(a) tilting pan with pouring lip designed to ensure safe movement of pan and also to facilitate transfer of hot foods to other receptacles;

(b) stainless steel lids (covers) hinged to open sideways and provide a working surface;

(c) operational controls sited conveniently for ease and safety of use;

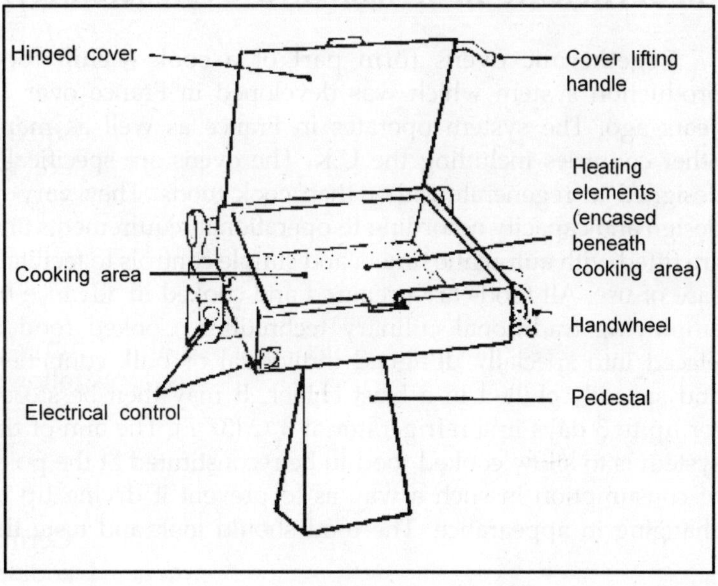

(d) flame failure and thermostatic cut-out devices;
(e) automatic safety devices: to cut off heat when pan is tilted, to cut off heat if thermostats fails,
(f) non-tilt and portable models are available.

Culinary uses

The bratt pan may be described as a multi-purpose piece of cooking equipment. Manufacturers claim that such equipment may be successfully used for: boiling; poaching; stewing; braising; shallow frying (sauté); deep frying; griddling; innovatory pot roasting; innovatory steaming; and also as a bain-marie. To have such versatility in one piece of equipment presents obvious major advantages to the catering industry. However when purchasing such equipment prospective buyers are well advised to consult recognized specialists and take advantage of the advisory services available, to ensure that the best possible model is obtained to meet the caterers own particular requirements.

REGETHERMIC REGENERATING OVEN (CABINET)

Regethermic ovens form part of a cook – chill food production system which was developed in France over 10 years ago. The system operates in France as well as many other countries including the U.K. The ovens are specifically designed to regenerate rather than cook foods. They vary in design and capacity according to operational requirements and are fitted with automatic timers and simple controls to facilitate ease of use. All foods are prepared and cooked in advance by employing traditional culinary techniques. Cooked food is placed into specially designed individual or bulk containers and speedily chilled in a blast chiller. It may then be stored for up to 3 days in a refrigerator at 3°C (37°F). The aim of the system is to allow cooked food to be reconstituted at the point of consumption in such a way as to prevent it drying up or changing in appearance. The food should look and taste the

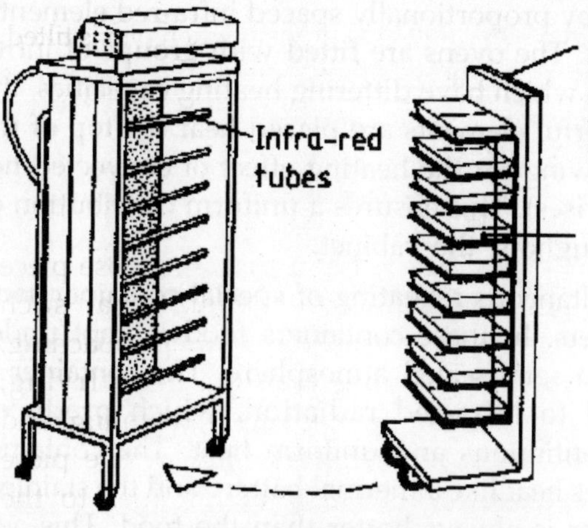

Example model of regethermic oven (cabinet)

same as when freshly cooked and retain as much nutritional value as possible.

The principle of regethermic regeneration

The method is based on two basic concepts:

1. The use of diffused infra-red rays operating on a predetermined wave length to achieve heat penetration requirements and characteristics. The exact

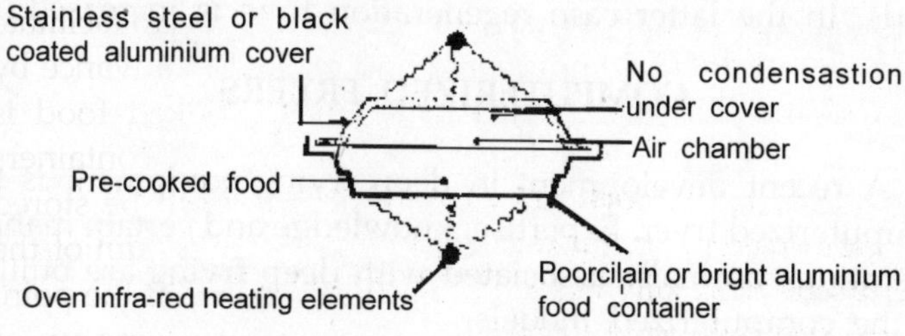

Sectional drawing of food container

degree of heat for regeneration within the oven is supplied by proportionally spaced infra-red elements, see below. The ovens are fitted with groups of infra-red tubes, which have differing heating capacities, the less powerful elements are placed near the top of the oven allowing for the heating effect of convected hot air (heat rises). This ensures a uniform distribution of heat throughout the cabinet.

2. The simultaneous reheating of special container sand their covers. In these containers food is kept under cover in a semi-sealed atmosphere. The container is subjected to infra-red radiation, which produced gentle, continuous and uniform heat. The container then stores heat like a thermal battery and the stainless steel cover is always hotter than the food. This acts to prevent condensation, keeping the food's flavour and aroma sealed within the container. The regethermic regenerating method uses radiated, conducted, and convected heat in varying proportions. The air chamber containing food is heated to serving temperature [60°-65°C (140°-149°F)].

Oven utility

As previously stated regethermic ovens are primarily designed to reconstitute pre-cooked, chilled foods, with an average regenerating time of 12–20 min. It is possible however to operate with freshly cooked foods and pre-cooked frozen foods. In the latter case regeneration time is increased.

COMPUTERIZED FRYERS

A recent development in deep frying equipment is the computerized fryer. Expertise, knowledge and certain manual operations normally associated with deep frying are built-in to the computerized models.

The 'fryer with a brain' may be programmed to control the following automatically:

(a) cooking times of a pre-selected range of products, to achieve the correct degree of cooking;

(b) the cooking temperatures, therefore eliminating the need for thermostats and calibration;

(c) high temperatures to ensure that the frying medium does not become too hot or reach flash point;

(d) low temperatures indicating by means of a signaling device when the oil/fat temperature drops excessively below 'set point';

(e) a shut-down effect if the fryer is not used over a pre-set period;

(f) a melt cycle to ensure safe melting of fat before the fryer automatically switches over to operating cycles;

(g) basket lifts, which operate automatically and independently to remove the products from the fryer once cooking is completed;

(h) holding timer, denoting that the holding period of the cooked product is over.

Controls are designed to be simple and offer a 'crisp' control to allow the operator to select preferred degree of crispness. The computer has a built-in test circuit to indicate that all systems are operational. Computers are programmed to cater for many standard menu items but manufacturers offer a programming service to develop a unit to suit individual needs.

Operational information

Information is fed into the computer from a super-sensitive probe, which is immersed in the frying medium. The probe passes information about temperature and rates of temperature change created by one or more of the following variables:

(a) initial oil/fat temperature;

(b) volume of food being fried;

(c) fryer efficiency and capacity;

(d) fryer recovery rate;

(e) quantity and condition of oil/fat;

(f) product temperature and water content.

By using this information the fryer is able to compute the exact cooking times required with the end of the cooking period being indicated by an automatic signalling device. When the computer needs servicing it is easily replaced by plugging in another computer control.

General factors

In addition to the special features outlined above, models maintain the general standards and refinements of modern fryers:

(a) compactly designed modular units;

(b) built-in filter to ensure removal of contaminants, moisture and fatty acids, therefore extending the life of the frying medium;

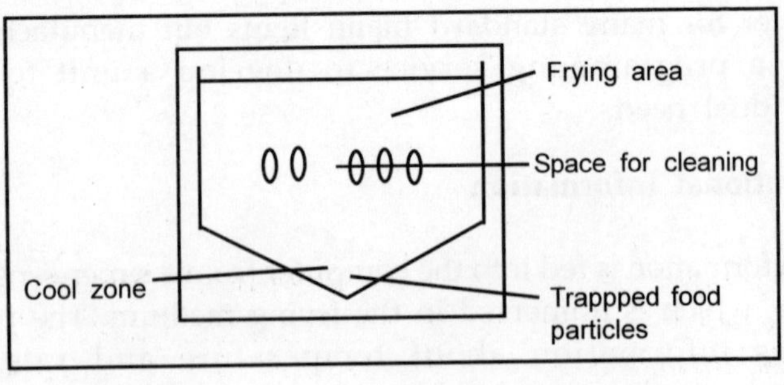

(c) cool zone that acts to keep solid particles form the heat source thus extending the life of the oil/fat and reducing the possibility of taste transfers;

(d) drain valve and oil receptacle to ensure safe and swift draining of the frying oil/fat.

A wide range of single or multi-product models are manufactured, designed of use with gas or electric services. Potential buyers should obtain first-hand advice from manufacturers about their particular catering requirements.

3

The Cooking of Food

Generally food is cooked when heat is transferred form a heat source, (e.g. stove) through to the exterior of foodstuffs by one or more of the following mechanisms:

(a) conduction

(b) convection

(c) radiation.

These processes function on the basis that where temperature differences exist heat will be transferred and directed towards areas of decreasing temperature. In order to understand how the heat transfer processes function it is helpful to know something of:

(a) the effect of heat upon food,

(b) the means by which heat is transferred through food to effect cooking.

HEAT AND HEAT TRANSFER (GENERAL PRINCIPLES)

All foods and all bodies of matter, e.g. pots and pans consist of atoms/molecules, which are constantly in motion. When heat is applied to foods or cooking vessels this motion is greatly accelerated and friction within the foods and cooking vessels greatly increased. The friction creates heat which passes through these materials by conduction. It should be noted that in most cases heat transfer within foods is primarily via the conduction process, however this is not the case where food is mainly or exclusively liquid, in these instances heat transfer is chiefly convective and rapid when the liquid is free to move; as is the case with stock, unthickened soups and gravies, etc. Where however foods that are initially liquid become thickened and semi-solid on heating, e.g. certain starch-thickened products, then convected heat is only important at the initial cooking stage. Once the food is thickened and the movement of liquid restricted the process of heat transfer by conduction within the food increases.

Cooking with conducted heat

The shallow frying of fish is a good example of how the conduction process transfers heat from a hot stove to a frying pan, through to the cooking oil and on to the outer surface of the fish. Cooking is continued as heat is transferred from the exterior through to the centre of the fish by conduction. At all stages of this operation the principles associated with heat and heat transfer described in the previous section apply. These stages include the heating of the cooking vessel, the oil and fish with the latter being changed from a raw to a cooked condition by the passage of conducted heat within the fish.

Cooking with convected heat

Convection occurs in gases and liquids, as opposed to solids because they can move more freely. As the gas (e.g. air) or liquids (e.g. water, stock, oil) are heated their structure expands and becomes less dense. In this condition the heated areas of the gas or liquid rise to be replaced by the cooler and denser gas or liquid present. This movement forms a convection current within the air or liquid. The warmed and less dense air/liquid gradually cools by giving up heat to the foods that are being cooked. On cooling this air/liquid becomes more dense and sinks again to complete the cycle.

The baking of pies illustrates the use of convected hot air as a heat transfer medium. The cold air within the oven is heated becomes less dense and rises. This is replaced by cooler denser air and the convection current of hot air is set in motion. The heated air gives up heat energy to the pies where it is absorbed passing through the pies by means of conduction to effect the well-known changes associated with baked products.

Similarly convection currents occur in liquids where they are used as heat transfer mediums during such methods as boiling, poaching, stewing, braising, steaming, and deep frying, in these instances water, moisture, stock or oil are used as the convection medium, but it should be noted that the temperature of these mediums is raised by heat conducted through the cooking vessel or steam generator.

Cooking with radiant heat

The grilling of food is an apt illustration of how emitted heat (energy) waves are transferred rapidly through the air and directed on to the exterior surface of foods. The heat energy is absorbed at the surfaces of food where it acts to generate friction. This in turn creates heat. Cooking continues from the exterior surface of the food through to its centre as heat energy travels by means of conduction. When cooking by radiant heat the energy waves heat the foods exterior surfaces only (as their ability to penetrate further is limited) and beyond this depth cooking is accomplished by conduction.

Summary

From these notes it is evident that in most cooking operations more than one mode of heat transfer is acting simultaneously. Also where foods are cooked by these conventional methods of heat transfer, heat penetration is seen to be relatively slow, commencing at the exterior of food and gradually traveling in wards by conduction.

COOKING METHODS IN COMMON USE

English term	French term	Heat transfer processes
To poach	Pocher	Conduction/convection
To boil/simmer	Bouillir/mijoter	Conduction/convection
To steam	Vaporizer	Convection/conduction
To stew	Etuver	Conduction/convection
To braise	Braiser	Conduction/convection
To pot-roast	Poeler	Conduction/convection
To deep-fry	Fire	Conduction/convection
To shallow fry	Sauter	Conduction
To grill	Griller	Radiation/conduction
To roast (oven)	Rotor	Convection/conduction
To roast (open-spit)		Radiation/conduction
To bake	Curie	Convection/conduction

THE EFFECTS OF COOKING ON FOODS

A previously stated, cooking methods involve the use of heat. These methods may differ in:

(a) how much heat or other radiant energy is applied to the food;

(b) the rate at which it is applied;

(c) the medium used for heat transfer, e.g. metal, water, fat, air;

(d) whether precautions are taken to prevent the loss of moisture or whether moisture is allowed to escape into the atmosphere.

The prime objective of cooking is to produce palatable, safe and attractive foods. However a particular food cannot necessarily be cooked by all the methods outlined in this section.

The effects described in the following sections occur during most cooking operations. The extent to which these changes occur depends upon the amount of heat energy transferred to the foods. Obviously the higher the temperature to which the food is heated and the longer the period of time for which the temperature is maintained, the greater the effects will be. As will be observed these effects will be modified by the medium employed for heat transfer, typically air (e.g. grilling, baking), water or steam (e.g. poaching, boiling, stewing) or fat (frying).

Cooking in fat creates an essentially dry environment that precludes reactions requiring water. When air is used it may be nearly dry or distinctly wet depending upon whether water is deliberately introduced (wet ovens) or derived only form the food being cooked. Cooking in water maximizes those reactions requiring the presence of water, e.g. gelling of starches and conversion of collagen in flesh foods to gelatin.

In the conventional methods of cooking there will be differences in temperature from the heat source to the centre of each item of food. The temperature differences are influenced by the nature and temperature of the heat source, the heat-conducting properties of nay materials between the heat source and the food (e.g. air, cooking vessel, pastry layer, sauce, stock, oil, etc.) and their thickness. It follows that different results will be obtained when using containers of different thermal conductivity. For example, for best results daubes (types of stew) are generally cooked in an earthenware pot (daubiere) to ensure steady even slow cooking, and certain copper-cooking vessels are often used for high speed cooking. Equally the extent of cooking-induced changes is always greater on the surface of a piece of food than at the centre; the greater the thickness of food, the greater the difference.

There are occasions when it is desirable to emphasize these difference e.g. production of a crisp brown skin on roast potatoes or French fries, the crackling on joints of pork, the semi-solid yolk and firm white of fried and soft boiled eggs. Equally there are occasions where such differences must be controlled, perhaps kept to a minimum. In principle temperature differences within a container can be kept to a minimum by agitation of the contents but in practice this might be undesirable where delicate foods could be broken up.

A common method to prevent differences in temperature is to use thin pieces or small portions of food which cook more quickly and more uniformly. For example, using sliced rather than whole potatoes, slicing joints of meat into steaks for grilling, frying or braising. It is possible to fry or grill entrecote steak so that the centre is cooked and the outside browned but acceptable, it would be quite impossible to fry or grill a whole counterfeit so that the centre was cooked sufficiently without severely overcooking the outside. This problem is overcome by using a lower external temperature and a longer cooking period as used in roasting instead of frying or grilling. The same is true of sliced and whole potatoes, which may be fried, roasted or boiled.

With certain cooking methods there will be a moisture content gradient as well as a temperature gradient caused by the evaporation of moisture from an exposed surface e.g. baking and roasting, which lead to different chemical reactions at the surface compared with the centre. Water lost form the surface may be partially replaced by water moving from the interior towards the surface. This water will carry with it soluble components, particularly sugars and amino acids, and these will be deposited at the surface as the water evaporates. Such substances are very susceptible to degrade and interact when heated, giving rise to yellow-brown or dark brown colours seen for example on the skin of roast potatoes, the crust of bread or the surface of roasted meats.

Poaching is often very brief and as it is a low temperature process its effects are mild. Frying and grilling are also brief operations that occur at much higher temperatures and are much more severe than poaching and boiling. Stewing is a long operation that permit certain changes to occur to a greater extent than during frying or grilling, and some to a lesser extent. For example, the extensive breakdown of some of the gristle is a very important feature of stewing is a wet method, the presence of water facilitating (hydrolytic) reactions such as collagen breakdown. In contrast baking and grilling are relatively dry methods, although steam may be present during baking and foods that are grilled naturally contain water that has been at least partially sealed in the food at the beginning of the process. Cooking by immersing food in fat and oils (deep frying) is also a relatively dry process because a substantial part of the water originally present is boiled away during the frying operation.

It is important to appreciate that, from a scientific point of view, the total time of the cooking operation begins with the first application of heat and ends with the consumption of the food. Therefore any period of holding food in a hot condition (e.g. hot plate) prior to service or any reheating process increases the extent to which changes occur. It is quite possible that the effects of holding hot may be greater than the effects of cooking and the total effect could be an undesirable overcooking. Accordingly it can be less harmful to cook or part-cook, cool, and reheat immediately prior to service. If food is held for nay length of time it is essential that a temperature is used that will prevent the growth of micro-organisms (e.g. bacteria and fungi).

The precise effects of cooking also depend upon the material being cooked. Fruits and vegetables for example differ considerably form flesh foods in structure and properties. Some of these differences are summarized in the table.

Differences in properties of foods from plant or animal origin

Foods of plant origin	Foods of animal origin
Usually *living* at the time of preparation in the kitchen	Tissues not living at this stage
Tissues have rigid cell walls	Tissues do not have distinct cell walls
Depend largely on turgor pressure* for raw texture-often served raw	Do not depend on turgor pressure for raw texture – rarely served raw
Protein content often low	Protein content often high
Starch content may be high	Starch content essentially low
Far content usually	Fat content variable, but usually higher

*Turgor pressure- gives raw foods of plant origin their firm and/or crisp texture before cell walls are damaged and water content is lost by preparation and cooking procedures.

The chemical and physical changes that occur during cooking operations are very complex and beyond the scope of this text but may be viewed as:

(a) physical changes in texture;

(b) chemical changes in flavour and odour;

(c) chemical changes in colour;

(d) chemical changes in nutritive value.

Since this text is not primarily concerned with nutritional aspects, the changes in nutritive value will not be discussed in detail. However everyone relies upon foods to supply the essential nutrients and it is desirable that nutrient losses should be minimized. In general the higher the temperature the longer the time of exposure to a particular temperature, the greater the will be the loss. Holding cooked food hot and reheating food are particularly destructive and should only be used when unavoidable. Flavour, odour, texture and colour may also be adversely affected by these practices.

N.B. Students interested in more detailed in-depth information concerned with the above changes should consult a comprehensive food science text (e.g. *An Introduction to Science for Catering and Homecraft Students* by O.F.G. Kilgour, Heinemann: London) however the following notes are included to highlight some of the changes which can be seen during the preparation and cooking of foods.

WHY DO WE COOK FOOD?

There are certain dished where some or all of the ingredients are eaten uncooked. However the majority of foods are cooked or re-heated from a cooked condition prior to service. Important reasons for cooking food are to destroy:

(a) many of the food spoilage micro-organisms;

(b) disease-producing pathogenic micro-organisms;

(c) parasites that were naturally/originally present.

Foods so treated are less susceptible to spoilage provided

that there is no contamination after cooking. Accepting that the destruction of dangerous organisms is one reason for the cooking of food, the question as to how raw salads and products, such as steak tartare, can be safe, needs to be answered. Fresh fruits and vegetables are relatively unlikely to contain dangerous micro-organisms or dangerous parasites, and provided they are thoroughly washed during preparation there is little risk. Intact fruit and vegetables are living tissues and relatively resistant to attack by spoilage organisms, but the risk of spoilage rises rapidly once they are bruised or cut.

The muscles of healthy animals are normally free form dangerous micro-organisms but raw meat is more susceptible to contamination with pathogenic and spoilage organisms than raw fruits and vegetables. Accordingly raw meat for products such as steak tartare must be very fresh and handled in conditions of strict hygiene. In the absence of a cooking stage such meat would have to be visually examined for the possible presence of parasites.

A second reason for cooking food is to soften it and make it easy to chew and digest. The gelatinization of starch, the breakdown of proteins and foods' structure are significant in this respect.

A third reason for cooking food is the creation of attractive and interesting ways used to obtain the nutrients required for a healthy life.

EXAMPLES OF THE EFFECTS OF COOKING UPON FOODS

Texture changes

When protein foods are subjected to cooking, changes in texture may occur which are referred to as setting, gelling and coagulating, some of these changes can be observed as they occur during the cooking of meat, fish, poultry or eggs, etc. during the poaching of eggs the effect of protein breakdown (denaturation) and coagulation can be clearly seen. These effects may be speeded up by the addition of an acid (vinegar) or salt to the poaching water. The effects of denaturation and coagulation on flesh foods cause shrinkage so that the water and juices are squeezed out. These juices often form the basis of gravies and sauces which accompany the foods. Gently cooked meat on the bone will shrink less than severely cooked meat, or meat off the bone, as the extent of shrinkage depends upon the severity of the heat process, and the time length of exposure. The fact that bone does not shrink during the cooking prevents the attached meat from shrinking freely.

Shrinkage of *muscle proteins** occurs at about 65°C. Meat, which is well cooked, will generally reach an internal temperature of about 80°C which is well above the shrinkage point, on the other hand meat which is cooked rare, e.g. beef will only reach an internal temperature of about 65°C and shrinkage will be less.

The setting/firming that occurs when cooked joints of meat are allowed to cool is associated with the cooling and setting of the fat that has dispersed throughout the meat during the cooking process.

Connective tissue proteins found in flesh foods as opposed to muscle proteins described above, behave differently during cooking, these proteins are commonly known as gristle (scientifically collagen, elastin and reticulin) Collagen when heated in liquid, e.g. stewed, breaks down to form water soluble gelatin. Any meat that is high in connective tissue, e.g. shin (20%) is best cooked by a slow, moist method to make it tender. Alternatively frying steak (3% connective tissue) can be cooked by a faster, dryer method and be tender. Tough stringy meat is due to a larger proportion of elastin and reticulin which do not break down during cooking but which can be removed from meat by careful butchery or broken up mechanically by mincing. The collagen found in fish is broken down much more easily than that found in meat and consequently many species of fish can be fried or

---

*Scientifically referred to as actin and myosin.

grilled. It is for this reason that fish muscle easily separates (flakes) during cooking because the connective tissue, collagen has denatured to form gelatin. Fish is suited to quick methods of cookery because it contains little connective tissue.

Cooking damages the structure of fruits and vegetables and causes a rapid loss of turgor pressure, water and water-soluble substances that were originally contained within the food structure are released and pass into air spaces between the fells. When there are extensive air spaces within the foodstuff loss or turgor pressure and replacement of air with water causes very marked changes in appearance and texture. This particular situation is illustrated by comparing cooked cabbage with raw cabbage, which when raw contains some 75% air by volume. Fruit such as apples contain some 25% air by volume but root vegetables such as carrots contain very little and accordingly there is less change in appearance and texture form this cause. The texture of vegetables and fruit is influenced by their composition as well as by cooking, apples, pears and potatoes show marked differences in texture after cooking, reflecting their different content of several carbohydrates.

TENDERIZING METHODS

These apply to the preparation and cooking of flesh foods. Before commenting on tenderizing methods applied in the preparation and cooking of flesh foods it is worth noting that the texture after cooking may vary depending on:

(a) type of animal-mammal, bird, fish , shellfish;

(b) age of animal-older muscles are tougher;

(c) location of muscle-muscles constantly in use tend to be tougher;

(d) fat content-generally the higher the fat content the juicer the texture;

(e) post-slaughter handling-incorrect handling can lead to tough flesh;

(f) cooking procedure-unsuitable cooking methods in relation to the type of flesh will lead to a tough product.

The modification of texture

(a) The slaughter and hanging of meat

The slaughter and immediate post-slaughter handling and chilling or freezing of meat influences its quality to a considerable extent. However the caterer has no direct control during this period and must rely upon his supplier. Many caterers purchase sides of meat that are a few days old and these improve in quality if hung at chill temperatures for a period of time, e.g. lamb 3-5 days and beef 10-17 days. Game is also hung for a substantial period of time.

During this period of handing, enzymes that are natural components of the flesh cause moderate breakdown of the tissues and produce meat of a more acceptable texture. Prolonged hanging also leads to flavour changes, particularly in game, it is most important that steps are taken during hanging to minimize microbial growth since this could lead to flavour taints or food poisoning, hence the use of chill temperatures, extreme cleanliness and sometimes ultra-violet lights in the store. Traditionally sides are hung from the Achilles tendon (in the ankle) but it is claimed that hanging form the aitch bone (in the thigh) gives more rapid tenderizing since the weight of the carcass pulls the muscle fibres apart. However, this method has less effect upon connective tissues than the traditional enzymic method.

(b) Tenderizing meat by adding enzymes

Softening (tenderization) occurs when enzymes are added to certain cuts/joints of meat for a period of time before cooking. Traditionally such enzymes are derived by introducing certain fresh fruits into the culinary product and the cooking process. Examples include meat cooked with fresh pineapple, figs and papaya. Now-a-days it is possible to purchase enzyme extracts, which can be sprinkled directly on to the meat's surface, thus avoiding the need for fresh tropical fruit and their flavouring effects.

It is important to appreciate that these added enzymes attack the meat form the outside and penetrate slowly. Further these enzymes are still active during the early stages of cooking and it is the outer layers that receive most heat and thus greater enzyme activity. Under such circumstances there is a very real risk of excessive softening (mushiness) on the outside and toughness at the centre.

An alternative approach is to inject the enzyme (typically papain derived from papaya) into the veins of the animal 30 minutes prior to slaughter. The heart and blood vessels then distribute the enzyme to all tissues of the animal (including the centre of large muscles that are to become large joints) prior to slaughter. After slaughter these enzymes operate in addition to those that were naturally present. If for some reason the animal is not slaughtered within approximately one hour of injection the enzyme is destroyed by the animals defence mechanisms and the animal suffers no harm. Carcases that have been so tenderized are available commercially. It is claimed that enzyme treatment before slaughter yields from a regular side of beef 70% of cuts suited to dry heat processing whereas without treatment only 30% of such cuts would be obtained.

Disadvantages of the treatment are over-tenderization of kidneys and tongue. It is said that the treated kidneys are well suited to uses where flavour rather than texture are required, and the tongue can be used provided the cooking process is more gentle than normal.

It is claimed that this enzyme treatment not only reduced inherent toughness but also reduced toughness induced by incorrect slaughter and post-slaughter cooling operations.

(c) Mincing

This breaks up the muscle of the connective tissue by mechanical means thus making chewing easier.

(d) Marinading

Marinades are essentially a mixture of oil and acid, which may be further flavoured by the addition of vegetables, herbs, seasoning, wine and/or spirit. Meat and fish can be marinaded in such mixtures for predetermined lengths of time to enhance flavour, in some instances effect colour changes, and generally tenderize the product. Any tenderizing effects are probably a result of alterations in acidity to a value that permits the protein to bind more water and dissolve some collagen into gelatin before cooking. These changes favour the continued conversion of collagen into gelatin during the subsequent cooking period.

(e) Pounding

Pounding is a milder form of mincing, which separates some of the fibres.

Flavour and odour changes

The chemistry of the flavour and odour of both raw and cooked foods is complex. Thousands of chemical compounds are known to possess specific odour and flavours and usually the smell or taste complex of any raw or cooked food contains at least 50 and possibly more than 500 such compounds, which are present in minute quantities. Changes of smell and taste that occur during cooking reflect the destruction of raw food compounds and the formation of new compounds in the cooked product. The majority of odour and flavour compounds are concentrated in the fatty components of food.

For example the fat content of meat plays an important role in contributing to juiciness after the cooking stage. During cooking the fat melts and passes through the tissues, with some passing into the drippings, also fat that is spread on the surface of met melts and diffuses through the tissues making it more succulent. In such operations the surface temperature is sufficiently high for some fat breakdown to occur which leads to the production of characteristic odour and flavour.

Following standard recipes and procedures helps to prevent unwanted reactions since the most likely causes of unpleasant odour and flavour are:

(a) incorrect recipe balance and procedure;

(b) using inferior quality ingredients;

Incorrect cooking, e.g. overheating, localized heating due to lack of agitation or movement, can lead to overcooked, burnt, tough and bitter tasting products due to a greater than normal destruction of the ingredients present.

Starch has the ability to bind flavour and odour compounds and reduce their intensity. The harshness of overspiced products can often be corrected by adding a small quantity of starch or starch-rich ingredient.

Colour changes

Changes in the colour of certain vegetables and fruit occur before cooking takes place and are a result of enzymic browning.

Enzymic browning

Certain vegetables and fruits turn brown or even darker in colour when cut or damaged and exposed to air (enzymic browning). This can be minimized as follows:

(a) Adding and acid (citric acid or lemon juice) - to adjust the pH value to a level that inhibits enzymic browning.

(b) Heating- this action may however cause undesirable changes in texture and flavour.

(c) Immersion in water or coating cut surfaces with a thin film of melted butter/oil-these procedures minimize browning because they exclude oxygen from the surfaces.

Common examples of products susceptible to enzymic browning are peeled apples, potatoes, bananas, and pears. In the case of fried mushrooms enzymic browning contributed beneficially to their colour.

THE EFFECTS OF PREPARATION AND COOKING UPON FOODS-COLOUR AND COLOUR CHANGES

The colour of food influences customer acceptability. Abnormal colours (discoloration) will rarely occur unless tainted ingredients and/or incorrect procedures are used.

Plant foods

The colouring pigment of green vegetables is chlorophyll. Unless it is partially degraded, chlorophyll is not soluble in water. Loss in colour through normal cooking methods is therefore low and usually unimportant. However on contact with acid (which may come form the vegetable itself) chlorophyll is converted to a brownish pigment which results in vegetable discoloration. Such discoloration can be prevented as follows.

Adding on alkali to the cooking water

Sodium bicarbonate – N.B. excessive additions will result in the destruction of vitamin C and thiamine and soften the vegetable's texture excessively.

Cooking in an open vessel

As most of the acids are volatile they are removed with the steam. In these cases it is wise to renew the cooking water for each batch of cooking. This method avoids the need to use sodium bicarbonate.

Traditionally the discoloration was avoided by adding copper in the form of a coin. This is not to be recommended since copper is poisonous.

Pale coloured fruits and vegetables (e.g. potato, parsnip, onion)

These contain substances, which when cooked in alkaline water, take on a yellow/cream colour. This colour change is not severe and therefore presents no problem in catering operations. If desirable the addition of a few drops of acid (lemon juice) to the cooking water avoids this colour change.

Strongly coloured fruits and vegetables (e.g. carrot, tomato, red pepper, pineapple, citrus fruits and radish)

These contain carotenoid pigments, which remain fairly stable on cooking. The result is a slight reduction in the colour intensity of such products.

The soft and stone fruits (e.g. strawberries, raspberries, cherries, etc.)

These contain red or purple pigments, which are water soluble. Such foods loose pigment if they are damaged then placed in cold water and also by cooking, if these pigments are treated with alkaline water they change form purple/red to blue/green, a reaction which is reversed by the addition of an acid (lemon juice). Normally the fruits themselves are sufficiently acidic and resist this change in the first instance.

Some of these fruits react with iron and other metals, e.g. tin, aluminium to produce bluish tints. Accordingly they should not be cooked in, or handled in utensils made of these metals.

A few vegetables contain red or purple pigments and should be treated similarly, the most common of these being red cabbage.

Beetroot

This contains unique pigments, which are water soluble and which show a slight colour change in alkaline water of no consequence to the caterer.

FOODS OF ANIMAL ORIGINS

The main pigments of meat and poultry are haemoglobin in the blood and myoglobin in the muscle. Meat normally contains far more myoglobin than haemoglobin since most of the blood is removed at slaughter. However, the chemical properties of haemoglobin are essentially identical to those of myoglobin and thus when blood is present or added e.g. to some stews) the changes that occur will be as described here for myoglobin.

The content of myoglobin varies, being higher in the dark muscles of meat, fish and poultry than in the pale muscles, this variation is clearly illustrated in crab, mackerel, pork and chicken,. Whatever he hue, fresh meat (i.e. not frozen) should have a relatively bright surface and duller interior. However, it must be noted that protein denaturation caused by freezing leads to a duller surface colour without necessarily indicating lower quality.

The colour produced after cooking depends upon the amounts of pigment present in the raw meat and the severity of the cooking process. Mild heating converts myoglobin to haemochrome which is pink and typical of lightly-cooked steak. Further heating converts haemochrome to a grey-brown hemochrome which is typical of a well-cooked steak.

Green colours should never be encountered but if they are they indicate gross microbial contamination and such meat is unit for human consumption.

Meat, fish and particularly shellfish also contain carotenoid pigments. When found in meat they impart a yellow colour to the fat. This is most frequently encountered with beef and implies that the meat is form an old animal and that it may therefore be tough. Carotenoids in fish are usually red or pink and examples include redfish, salmon, and tuna. Similar colours may also be encountered in crustacean shellfish, but this type of fish may also contain blue carotene-protein complexes. Cooking causes the complex to break and give rise to the more typical orange-red corotenoid colour, e.g. lobster shell turns from bluey black to red/orange on cooking.

Milk, dairy products and egg yolks are coloured mainly by carotenoids and the colour intensity mainly reflects the carotenoid content of the feed the animal received. High pigmentation is not necessarily a sign of high quality.

Discoloration that may be encountered in fish and shellfish includes a rusty colour on the cut surface of white fish fillets and a black colour (black spot) on prawns and shrimps. The former is caused by incorrect bleeding of the fish after capture and the latter by incorrect handling of the prawns which permits an enzymic browning type of reaction to occur. There is little the caterer can do except reject the material and, if necessary, change supplier.

PREPARED FOODS

Many foods take on a yellow or brown colour as a result of cooking. Typically the reactions responsible are known as non-enzymic browning and are chemically complex. The colour-producing ingredients are typically sugars and amino acids or protein, but may be modified by other ingredients particularly acids. Often colours of this type are considered desirable, e.g. caramel, toast, roasted coffee but on occasion they may appear when not required, e.g. in white sauces, fruit juices and typically indicate over-heating, although typical of prepared foods these reactions may occur in, for example, cooked meat, and make an important and desirable contribution to the colour particularly of the paler meats after cooking, e.g. pork and chicken.

One typical reaction in which proteins may participate is called non-enzymic or Maillard browning, this reaction gives the characteristic brown colouring and flavour of cooked foods, meat in particular, and although some nutritive value is lot in the process, it is offset by the increased attractiveness of the food and, therefore, its greater palatability.

The mechanisms by which culinary products are thickened to varying degrees can be sub-divided into three separate processes: starch thickening; protein coagulation; and emulsification.

STARCH THICKENING

Starches may be isolated from many plants, and when pure they are white, odourless, tasteless powders. Often instead of pure starches, starch-rich materials, e.g. cereals and pulses, are used as thickeners and these may be slightly coloured and have characteristic but acceptable odours and flavours. Because starch is a major component these starch-rich materials behave similarly but not identically to pure starches. Starches are commonly available from the kitchen stores in the following forms.

The nature of commodities commonly used as sources of starch

White flour	Produced from wheat. Also contains protein and fat	
Cornflour	Purified maize starch	
Arrowroot	A powered root consisting almost exclusively of starch. Sometimes referred to as a fecula or fecule	
Tapioca	Powdered cassava root, also a fecula and as a thickening agent very similar to arrowroot.	
Fecule	Potato powder, perhaps the commonest fecula	
Starchy vegetables	Potato is a fresh vegetable has a much higher moisture content and therefore lower starch content than the powder described above.	
	Split peas	Starch-rich pulses also containing
	Lentils	Protein and a little fat.
Farinaceous materials	Also known as cereals; include barley and rice grains. Protein and fat are also present	
Special starches	Starches isolated form plants which in some cases are chemically treated to meet particular requirements. Almost pure starches. Examples include waxy maize starch, waxy rice starch, pregelatinized starches, freeze-thaw resistant starches.	

4

Grooming Procedures for Kitchen Staff

BOYS

Bathing	: Employees must bathe daily to get rid of body odour
Uniform	: Please follow the instruction given in uniform section in the staff manual.
Facial hairs	: Clean shaved no visible facial hairs.
Socks	: Black/white only
Shoes	: Sport shoes with rubber sole
Perfume/after shave	: None
Rings	: None
Other jewellery	: No earrings. No watches, chains only if they are hidden from view.
Nails	: Neatly cut
Hair cut	: Hair should be above collars, hair should not fall on ears and side burns should be half the length of the ears.

GIRLS

Bathing	: Employees must bathe daily to get rid of body odour
Uniform	: Please follow the instruction given in uniform section in the staff manual.
Socks	: Black/white only
Shoes	: Sport shoes with rubber sole
Perfume	: None
Rings	: None
Other jewellery	: Small earring (Studs). No watches, chains only if they are hidden from view.
Nails	: Neatly cut and shaped
Hair	: Neatly tied back there should be no following of hair on face.

KITCHEN STAFF UNIFORM

The chef's uniform is white is colour, made of heavy duty cotton with white and black checks trousers. Employees are expected to wear the chef uniform provided to them in the first year, which includes:

- Full sleeves white chef coat
- Black and white checked trousers
- A large white apron tied around the waist
- A red scarf around the neck. (except head chef with black scarf)
- A chef cap (will be provided by head chef)
- Socks: Black/white only
- Shoes: Sport shoes with rubber sole

Please note: Uniform should be worn properly, uniform pocket should not be stiffed with personal belonging like combs, wallets or other personal articles.

KITCHEN HEIRARCHY

Head chef
Bharat Saini

↓

Sous chef
Jitin Neon

↓

Chef de partie
Aman Arora

↓

Commis chefs
Richa, Malhotra, Ashit Taneja, Manik Sethi,
Angadbir Singh Jaspal, Sahil Mohanti,
Aanchal Uppal

JOB DESCRIPTION

SOUS CHEF

Department : Kitchen

Reports to : Head chef

Job summary, duties and responsibility

Some chef to assist in the day to day running of the kitchen, supporting the Head Chef, deputizing in his absence, and ensuring that first class services is provided at all times

Your main responsibilities will be to support the head chef in the day to day running of the kitchen, and deputizing in his absence

The position calls for individuals with the ability to provide on-going training, supervising and coaching of other junior chefs in the group to ensure they are working effectively and that the required standards are maintained at all times.

The position requires responsible individuals with good attention to detail and strong organizational and supervisory skills.

This is the brief job profile for a Sous Chef and no way states that these are the only duties to be preformed by the respective staff.

CHEF DE PARTIE

Department : Kitchen

Reports to : Head Chef & Sous Chef

Job summary, duties and responsibility:

Delegate roles to Commis Chefs, ensuring optimal productivity, supervision and training where necessary.

To report any illness, hazards or unsatisfactory behaviour to the Head Chef.

To be fully aware of and adhere to all Health and Safety, Fire and Food Hygiene legislation and procedures, ensuring that Commis Chef also comply.

Should be able to plan, prepare and set up and provide quality services in all areas of food production.

Maintain cleanliness and sanitation in the kitchen.

Must be well versed health conscious methods of food preparation

This *is the brief job profile for a Chef de Partie and no way states that these are the only duties to be performed by the respective staff.*

COMMIS CHEF

Department : Kitchen

Reports to : Head Chef & Sous Chef & Chef de partie

Job summary, duties and responsibility

Commis chefs will be requested to work in all areas of the kitchen and have a basic understanding of all areas. Maintain a high standard of Hygiene and Safety in the kitchen.

To help in preparing mis en place in accordance with recipe and the hygiene regulations

To maintain a good working relationship with colleagues at all times

To assist in any area of the kitchen where requested.

This is the brief job profile for a Commis Chef and no way states that these are the only duties to be performed by the respective staff.

SOUS CHEF

Knowledge : should have knowledge of kitchen operations.

Experience : Should have 1 year working experience in kitchen during supervised work experience

Skills:

- Should have the ability work under pressure
- Professionally trained in culinary skills
- A great team player
- Committed and dedicated for the success of the event

CHEF DE PARTIE

Knowledge : Should have knowledge of kitchen operations.

Experience : Should have one year working experience in kitchen during supervised work experience

Skills:

- Should have the ability work under pressure
- Professionally trained in culinary skills

- A great team player
- Committed and dedicated for the success of the event

COMMIS CHEF

Knowledge : Should have knowledge of kitchen operations.

Experience : Should have 1 year supervised work experience

Skills:

- Should have the ability work under pressure
- A great team player
- Committed and dedicated for the success of the event

FOOD PICK UP PROCEDURES

It is the duty of the head Chef to ensure that every thing goes well in the kitchen. Also that the guest receives their order in time as well as right item is served to the right guest. To ensure this the following procedure will be followed.

The bus boy will bring the KOT to the kitchen handing over to the kitchen staff which will mention clearly what dish to be served to which guest and the table number, also mentioning the special request if any. Then the food item will be carried by the bus boy from the kitchen to the table.

DISCIPLINARY AND GRIEVANCE PROCEDURES (RULES AND REGULATIONS)

To have a good working atmosphere the management team has lay down certain rules and regulation to ensure all the employees are treated equally and no injustices are done to any of them. All the employees are expected to follow these rules and regulations:

- The Head of the Departments will maintain attendance record of all the employees in respective departments of the trainings as well as on the day of event.

- Time keeping is very essential, late comers will be marked absent, no excuses will be tolerated.
- In case employee is absent but is medically not well has to give the medical certificate in the following week and hence the person will not be marked absent. But if there is no good reason for absenteeism please do not expect any helps from the management team in terms of attendance record.
- Please inform Human Resource Manager if medically unfit, prior to any session.
- At work whether it is training, briefing or live event NO playing or using of cell phones will be allowed. It is suggested that please do not bring your cell phones at all. Employees will not be allowed to use cell phones even in breaks.
- In case somebody is caught using the cell phones, his/her cell phone will be taken by the HR manager and will be returned only after event is over and clearance is done.
- Dinking while on duty/coming to work drunk will not be accepted and disciplinary action will be taken against him/her.
- Complains whether related to unfair working conditions or staff attitude/behaviour should be refer to the respective head of department or human resource manager, it will be then written down on complain sheet and appropriate actions will be taken.
- It is responsibility of each and every employee working for the event to follow health and safety regulations, remember it is for your own safety.
- Using slang or abusive language or inappropriate body language will not be tolerated. Employee found guilty will be asked to leave the premises right there and then and will be marked absent for the day.
- It is the duty of each and every staff member to follow

the instructions given by the management team.

- In case employees found guilty for stealing guest, colleagues or club property, very strict disciplinary action will be taken against him/her.
- Please note leaving from work without notifying the HOD will not be accepted.

Please remember that the Management Team is always there to help, staff can trust upon us.

KITCHEN TRAINING TIME PLAN

Kitchen training will be held exactly one week before the event.

10.00 am	The entire Kitchen Team will be asked to come at Unitech Country Club Kitchen
10:15 am	Attendance will be taken by Head Chef
10:30 am	Training will start, Detailed information about the menu and the recipes will be provided along with personal hygiene, Disciplinary Procedures, Fire Safety procedures will be discussed.

There is no end time mentioned for the training as it entire depends on Menu preparations.

Training will be held by Head Chef and Human Resource Manager.

KITCHEN ACTIVITIES ON THE DAY OF EVENT

1. Delivery of food items
2. The Head Chef takes inventory check.
3. Opening checklist.
4. Storage to appropriate areas; raw meat and other food items to be stored separately.
5. Equipment check.
6. Attendance of the employees will be taken

7. Clean the vegetables.
8. Initial mise-en-place.
9. Cooking begins.
10. Final mise-en-place before service begins.
11. Soup Service.
12. Starter Service
13. Main course service.
14. Dessert service
15. Tea/coffee service
16. Staff meal.
17. Cleaning the kitchen surfaces and equipment
18. Winding up procedure
19. Closing check list
20. Attendance of the employees will be taken
21. Close the kitchen.

EXTINGUISHER

When and how to use a fire

1. *Fight or flee*

Your safety is the most important consideration. Do not fight the fire if:

- There is considerable heat
- There is significant smoke or fumes
- There is any possibility that you will be trapped by the fire

2. *Call the fire department*

You or someone else should call the fire department or the fire emergency number provided to you before fighting the fire.

3. Choose the correct extinguisher

Extinguishers may handle more than one type of fire. Check the instructions on the extinguisher for the appropriate classification or symbol.

A. **"Ordinary combustibles"**, wood, paper, household rubbish, cloth, rubber, and many plastics

B. **Flammable liquids** – oils, greases, tars, oil-based paints, lacquers, flammable gases, and some plastics

C. "**Energized**" (plugged in) electrical equipment household appliances televisions and radios, computers, wiring and fuse boxes or circuit breakers.

D. Combustible metals-magnesium, potassium, sodium and titanium

4. Using the extinguisher

Pull the pin — Point the nozzle away from you, release the locking mechanism

Aim low — Hold the extinguisher upright, aim at the base of the fire

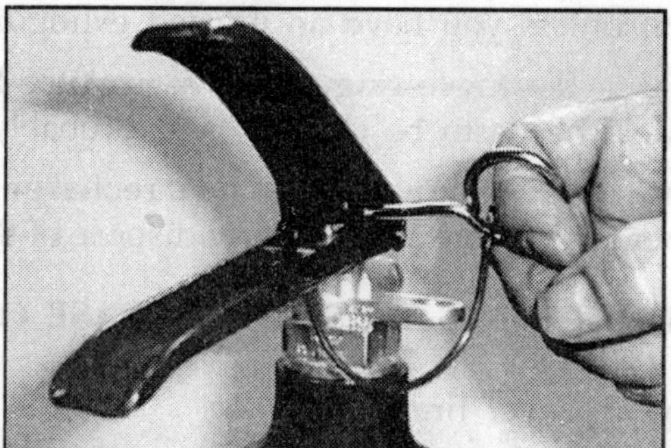

Squeeze the trigger	Remember that when the extinguishing agent comes out the nozzle it may do so with considerable force and noise-be prepared
Sweep side-to-side	Sweep the nozzle from side-to-side, driving the fire back. As the fire closest to you is extinguished you may move forward, but continue the sweeping motion

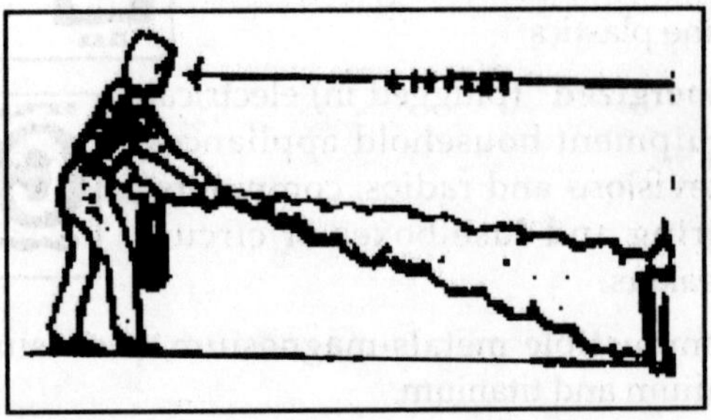

5. *After the fire*

Fires frequently re-ignite. Have the fire-department or your company fire brigade check the fire. If available, get another fire extinguisher to the site. Fire extinguishers are discharged very rapidly. You may not be able to deal with re-ignition unless you have an unused extinguisher.

Recharge the fire extinguisher. No matter how long it was sued, it needs to be checked and probably recharged.

If the fire extinguisher is not rechargeable, get a replacement (new) one and properly dispose of the used one.

INSTRUCTIONS TO STAFF IN CASE OF FIRE

If you discover fire:

- Operate the nearest fire alarm call point by breaking the glass.

- Use the available fire extinguisher only if you are confident enough to handle it without making nay kind of damage to yourself.

Evacuation procedure

In case of evacuation, please assemble to the assembling point which is car park in front of the hotel and report to the human resource manager who will be taking attendance to make sure every one is out of the club.

While evacuating

- Do not use lifts
- Do not delay by collecting personal belongings
- Do not re enter the building until informed to do so by fire officer
- Switch off all the equipments your were using

Please remember

If fire alarm siren sounds for 45 seconds and then stops

This is an alert for evacuation

But if the alarm siren sounds for longer then 45 seconds

Evacuate immediately

ACCIDENTS

Accidents are unwanted events that can cause minor or major injuries, loss or damage therefore it is suggested to all employees to follow all the rules and regulations set by the management team so that accidents can be avoided. If anyone meet with and accident it is suggested please report to the respective head of department (No matter how small the injury is).

Please remember management team has put your safety as their priority.

How accidents take place?

It is generally caused due to the carelessness done either by your colleagues or by yourself. For example

- Blocking passages with equipments
- Leaving cupboard doors and drawers open
- By not using safety devices while grinding or slicing
- Picking up broken glass bare handed
- Fiddling with hot oil/water/or any utensil
- Knifes are the major source of accidents.

Types of accidents

- Cuts
- Falls
- Burns
- Electric shocks

Precautions to prevent accidents

- Never play with knifes
- Do not leave knife in sink
- Handle broken glass with care
- Open tin cans with cutter only
- Do not run with knife in your hands
- Keep floor dry, clean and grease free
- Do not clean electrical appliances unless unplug from the socket
- Do not sprinkle water on hot oil.
- Concentrate on your work and follow instructions while operating appliances

First Aid Box

Please report all the accident to the head of department irrespective of its effectiveness

- Each and every employee should know the location of first aid box
- Ensue that the first aid box is kept at the same place after use.
- Always call first aider of your team or any member of management team.
- Please remember management team has put your safety as their priority.

5

Applied Hygiene in Our Kitchen

WHY HYGIENE IS SO IMPORTANT?

Foods badly preserved, conserved or prepared = extreme danger

Micro-organisms can develop in or on,

- Raw aliment
- Cooked aliment

They can provoke:

- Damages and deterioration of food quality
- Infections (diarrhoea, vomiting)
- Food poisoning
- Chronic and debilitating illness

Youngsters, pregnant women and older people are particularly sensible!

Most important hygienic routine

Hygiene is protecting aliments against,

- Contamination (micro-organisms)
- Development of micro-organisms

Prevention: micro-organisms enter our kitchen through,

- Contaminated aliments
- Dirty utensils
- Man
- Animals and insects
- Plants, soil
- Air

PROTECTING ALIMENTS

- During storage
- During preparation

Always maintain a very strict cleanliness standard

- On your person (hair, hands, nails, body and clothes)
- Operation equipment (mixer, grinder, kitchen utensils)
- Installations (refrigerator, sinks, oven, working space, ventilation)
- Locals (floor, walls, lockers, litter space).

WHEN MICRO-ORGANISMS ARE BECOMING DANGEROUS?

When they are reproducing in large number

Development of micro-organisms depends on

- Aliment's composition
  - Water content
  - Protein content
- Other nutritive elements such as vitamins and mineral salts
  - Temperature
  - Acidity (pH)

- Time
  - 0 minutes - nothing
  - 15-20 minutes - hundreds
  - 3 hours - thousand
  - 6 hours - millions
  - 12 hours - billions

WHICH MICRO-ORGANISMS AND PARASITES ARE DANGEROUS?

Frequent and recognized to provoke intoxication, vomiting or diarrhea

Bacteria	**Sources**
Salmonella	- Raw poultry
- Egg	
- Raw meat	
- Fresh milk produces	
- Crustaceans	
- Dirty and humid surfaces	
Staphylococcus	- Infected wound or pustule
Clostridia	- Raw meat
- Soil	
Bacillus cereus	- Cereals (rice)
Campilobacteries	- Raw poultry
Listeries	- Cheese (crust)
	- Raw meat

OTHER MICRO-ORGANISMS AND PARASITES

Sources

Less known and chronic * Beans

Mildew and its toxins
* Nuts, hazelnut
* Peanuts
* Cereals

Parasites

Limited in Europe but very serious and chronic
* Raw meat
* Liver
* Crustacean
* Some sausage's products

IN OUR KITCHEN, PREVENTION IS FUNDAMENTAL

Always, chose your equipment and utensils
- Stainless steel
- Hard plastic
- Avoid wood

Advantages

- Easy to clean, dry and maintain
- No fissure

Maintain cleanliness

- Chinaware, pots
- Kitchen utensils
- Sponge, clothes, kitchen hand towel
- Refrigerator, freezer

Attention

- Flies and other insects = Danger
- Always cover food container
- No domestic animals in the kitchens

TO PREVENT CONTAMINATION AND PROBLEMS IN RAW OR COOKED FOOD

Purchasing

- Always select best quality

Transport

- Fast, isolated bag or special container for refrigerated or frozen food

Storage

- Fresh storage maximum 20°Centrigrate (day to day)
- Cold storage maximum 4 to 5°Centrigrade
- Freezer for frozen good and ice cream

Preparation

- Clean thoroughly and rapidly

Service

- Fast at fresh temperature

Food leftovers

- For tomorrow's consumption, always keep in refrigerator in covered container

PREVENTION OF CONTAMINATION AND PROBLEMS IN COOKED AND HOT FOOD

Heat destroys micro-organisms

- Heat
- Pasteurization (milk)
- Sterilisation (canned food)

Cooking temperature must reach at least 70°Centgrigarde, including heart of food item

After heating and cooking AVOID all possible contacts with raw aliments

Conservation

For later consumption (i.e. stews)

- Fast cooling and chilling (i.e. on ice)
- Refrigerate immediately, in covered container

Re-heating

- Fast but enough heat to be provided (70°Centrigadre)
- Microwave oven heats without sterilizing: check manual of operation

Defrosting frozen goods

- Always through refrigeration or microwave

CONSERVATION AND FOOD HANDLING

1. Fish & seafood, storage, and method of conservation

FISH

With new and more sophisticated mean of transport and storage possibilities, it is now a day very easy to receive and keep fresh fish.

However and depending on countries and its level of sophistication in terms of transport, serious means of hygiene and temperature level have to be implemented.

The optimal nutritional composition of most of the fishes, bring this category into a very precious food value around the world. Fish breeding takes more importance every day and permits feeding of more and more people worldwide.

Soft water and sea water fishes

Fish who lives in both water such as eel, salmon, or sturgeon is called migratory fish, to classify them, we take in consideration their region of birth.

Round and flat fishes

Round fishes have 2 fillets, flat fish have 4 fillets.

Fat or lean fishes

Among fat fishes we can count, per example, eel, salmon, anchovy, mackerel, sardine, tuna fish, etc.

The biggest variety consists in lean fishes, such as sole, bar seabass, pike, cod, etc.

The quality

We recognize fish quality with the following signs,

- Fish smells agreeably, as the oceans.
- Eyes are clear, shiny and well curved.
- Scales are strongly kept and closed to the skin
- Skin is humid, possess a high degree of viscosity but should never be sticky
- Gills are generally clear red
- Flesh is flexible when you touch it, but takes immediately its original position.

Storage

Live fishes will be kept in tanks. Special care should be given to,

- Provide enough air
- Provide enough water circulation
- Check that water temperature is steady from 9 to 12°C

- Clean regularly the tank

Dead fishes will be kept in refrigerated fish drawers or kept on crushed ice, belly down, in holed trays, permitting evacuation of melted water from fish belly, and keeping maximum refrigeration. Crushed ice to be changed regularly.

Methods of conservation

- Refrigeration
- Freezing
- Smoking
- Salt
- Brine
- Sterilization/pasteurisation

Caviar

This very special gourmet item, is prepared form the eggs of different sorts of sturgeon such as:

- Fish
- Beluga
- Sevruga
- Oscietre

Salt is the conservation element. The famous "Malossol" denomination is only accorded to caviar with a maximum of 4% content of salt.

CRUSTACEAN

Seafood are animal without vertebra, protected by a shell. In every moulting this animal is getting rid of its old shell to allow dilatation. At this particular moment crustacean are the tastiest.

Their five pairs of feet are a characteristic from this animal, generally the first pair is doted with claws.

There is more than a thousand king of crustacean.

Here is a list of the most famous,

Form the ocean

- Shrimp
- Marine lobster
- Crab
- Lobster
- Etc.

From the river

- Royal crawfish
- Swamp crayfish
- Tasmanian crawfish

SEAFOODS AND MOLLUSCS

Seafood and mollusc are also animals without vertebra. Most of them are coming from the sea, very few of them live in soft water or on land.

The most important are,

Seashells

- Oysters
- Mussels
- Scallops

Most important: All seashells should be hermetically close at buying time. The open ones are basically dead and unusable.

Snails

- Vineyard snail
- Seasnail

- Bulot

Octopus

- Calamares
- Seiche

Other kinds

- Sea urchin
- Palourde

2. Meat, storage and method of conservation

MEAT

Under butchery meat we can classify,

The bovine species

- Veal
- Beef (young calf)
- Beef (castrated)
- Bull
- Cow

The pork species

- Suckling pig
- Young pig
- Pig

The ovine species

- Milk fed lamb
- Lamb
- Sheep
- Mutton

The caprine species

- Goat
- Wild goat.

The horse species

- horse
- colt

All slaughtered animals, except rabbits, are immediately controlled by the "service of inspection for meats". They are thoroughly examined to control their consumption aptitude, then stamped with one of the following;

- Meat apt for consumption
- Imported meat apt for consumption
- Horse meat apt fort consumption
- EC stamps.

Nutritive values

Meat is a precious protein's provider and provides minerals such as iron or vitamin B. The offal and especially liver are the richest in vitamins, but also have a high percentage of cholesterol content.

- The meat protein (albumin) have a high content of amine acids, which is why even in small quantity, they have a high value which gives the advantage of covering the basic proteins' needs.
- Grease value is very diverse according to the different meats
- Meat (except liver) barely contain carbohydrates

Meat quality

Criteria for meat quality are very different according to the cooking needs. At the buying time the following steps have to be observed:

- Meat/bone percentage
- Colour
- Grease percentage
- Fibre's structures
- Cartilage's composition

Preparation and storage

Meat being an easily and fast damaged ingredient, a careful preparation is an unavoidable condition to handle it,

- Meat and its entire derivative, should be stored between 0 and 2° centigrade
- Hang all different kind of meat or store them separately in hygienic container in the refrigerator.
- Meat losing rapidly weight during storage, it is recommended to portion it and vacuum pack. This type has proved to be efficient except for pork meat.
- Vacuum packed conservation is effective only if it is accompanied with adequate refrigeration or immediate freezing.

Accessory product of slaughtering

By accessory product of slaughtering we understand the following,

- Feet
- Head
- Tripe
- Liver
- Sweet bread
- Tail
- Tongue
- Kidney
- Etc.

Processed meat product

All processed meat products are considered as delicatessen. Different process are used for this type of meat product such as, salted, smoked, dried, roasted or cooked, filling for sausage, "charcuterie", canned, marinated, pates, ground meat and others.

The "charcuterie" divided in three categories,

- Scalded sausage
- Sausage of cooked meat
- Sausage of raw meat

3. Poultry, storage and method of conservation

POULTRY

As poultry we understand all animal domestically raised. They produce eggs and meat for human consumption. Flesh is very rich in proteins, well digested and have a low fat content (when served skinless).

We divide poultry in two groups, according to flesh colour,

White flesh poultry

- Chick
- Cock
- Cornish hen
- Cereal/seed fed chicken (Bresse)
- Chicken
- Fowl
- Turkey
- Turkey-hen
- etc.

Best poultry quality is given by young animal, well fed, with flexible breastbone, and clear red crest. Feet are still smooth, nails and beak sharp, and masculine species have a short ergot.

Darker flesh poultry

- Duck
- Duckling
- Gosling, simpleton (oison)
- Guinea-fowl
- Pigeon
- Greenhorn
- etc.

Generally criteria of quality are the same as for white flesh poultry. Feet membrane for aquatic species is still easily ripped off, and the neck is very soft and malleable.

Storage

The poultry meat being an easily and fat damaged ingredient, it is very important to keep it fresh at a temperature of 1-3° Centigrade at a low humidity rate not exceeding 70%. Maximum storage, one week.

4. Game, storage and method of conservation

GAME

Game is a generic name, which apply for feathered or furry species. Living in freedom in the forests, hunting reserve or fields and is apt for human consumption. Numerous species of game are to be noted such as, dear, wild boar, antelope, springbok, roebuck, reindeer, hare, pheasant, partridge, etc.

Furry game species

They are subdivided in;

Cervide game

- Roebuck
- Stag
- Chamois
- Reindeer

Dark flesh game

- Wild boar
- Bear

Rodent game

- Hare
- Wild rabbit

As soon as it is slaughtered the furry game, is cleaned of its bowels by the hunter and left hanged head down (still in its skin) between 8 to 12 days in a refrigerated area. This process is referred as "faisandage" or "mortification".

Game meat quality

Flesh quality depends on few factors,

- Age of the animal (coarse fibre features = older animal)
- Quantity of ingested food (enough food = better flesh)
- The impact of the bullet (the ideal hit is in the shoulder so that legs, lion are well preserved)
- Using the correct storage conditions (see above)

Storage

Game is generally featuring a stronger, firmer and more muscular fixture than domestic animals, storage required being adequate. (See above).

A slightly tart flavour is a plus, for game lover and this is due basically to correct storage condition (mortification).

Feathered game

This category is normally poor in fat content except for wild duck. Flesh has a strong game flavour. This is the "in" game especially, duck and pheasant. Only young-feathered game is tender.

Storage

- Store vacuum packed with date indication
- Freeze at minus 18° Centigrade
- Hang without feathers (except sea feathered game) this process is called "faisandage" (mortification).

Few feathered game

- Wild duck
- Wood cock
- Partridge
- Pheasant
- Quail
- Wild goose
- Snow partridge
- Etc.

5. Vegetable and fruits, storage & humidity requirement

VEGETABLES

Vegetables are essential for the human body. Everyday our body needs substances given from vegetables such as vitamins, mineral elements, carbo-hydrates, proteins, water and fibres.

Storage

If possible, we should always eat and serve fresh vegetables in our hotel restaurants. They have to be protected form light, heat, other type of odours and kept in a cool environment.

Some choice of vegetables

- Garlic
- Artichoke
- Asparagus
- Aubergine (eggplant)
- Beat root
- Celery
- Cauliflower
- Brussels sprout
- Chinese cabbage
- Cabbage
- Heart of palm
- Cucumber
- Spinach
- Pumpkin zucchini
- Fennel
- Accra
- Lettuces
- Salads
- Corn
- Onions
- Shallot
- Green peas
- Leek
- Beans

- Peas
- Green pepper
- Red peeper
- Yellow pepper
- Potatoes
- Radish
- Black radish
- Horseradish
- Rhubarb
- Tomatoes
- Iceberg lettuce
- Etc, etc

POTATOES

Everybody knows that potato was imported from South America. What is less known is that potato is from the same family as tomato and eggplant.

Potato is one of the most important and precious food items for human consumption

Potato content:

About	15 to 20%	carbohydrates
About	2%	proteins
About	75%	water
About	2%	lipids

Beside, it contain Vitamin C, (200 grams of potato cover 40% of the daily need for the human body), mineral elements such as calcium, sodium, potassium, iron, iodine, and Fluor.

Storage

The best storage method is to keep them between 4 to 6° centigrade, with air humidity factor of about 85 to 95%.

Starched vegetable

For along time in Europe, starch vegetables were considered a not too elegant food for their filling qualities. In modern time, fine culinary cooking rediscovered the quality of starch vegetables (dried or fresh).

They have the most value in vegetal proteins and give the human body B vitamins, minerals such as iron, potassium, and phosphor as well as an important intake of fibres.

Starched vegetables are classified in 3 important categories, such as:

BEANS

- White bean
- Borlotti bean
- Cannelloni bean
- Kidney bean
- Brittany bean
- Lima bean
- Midget bean
- Black bean
- Red bean
- Broad bean
- Soya bean
- Black soya
- Pinto bean

PEAS

- Yellow peas
- Green peas
- Chick peas
- Etc.

LENTILS

- Green lentils
- Egyptian pink lentils
- Yellow lentils
- Indian brown lentils
- Dark puy lentils
- Etc.

Storage

It is necessary to store them in a dry and ventilated environment, away from light. Before cooking, it is necessary to soak them between 8 to 12 hours.

SOYA PRODUCT, TOFU

Tofu being fabricated from the milk of the yellow Soya' seeds, has practically no flavour on its own, it has then, a fabulous adaptability in accompanying any dishes.

Tofu has a high protein and precious fat acids' content. It is recommended to combine with other type of foods because it does not content any fibres. Tofu is cholesterol free.

Other type of soya products

- Soya yoghurt
- Soya sauce
- Soya milk

MUSHROOMS

To grow, mushrooms need heat and humidity. Eatable and poisonous mushrooms grow together, which is why a thorough knowledge of the different kinds is absolutely necessary to pick them.

Warning

- If you pick your own wild mushrooms, always have them checked by a connoisseur.
- Date, name of the mushroom quantity and the name of the producer should always appear on the package.
- Do not keep fresh mushrooms too long, process immediately.
- Wash mushroom just before processing
- Soak dried mushrooms for one hour before processing, do not use this water for cooking
- Do not reheat mushroom's dishes.

Few mushroom type

- Paris mushroom
- Cepes
- Shiitake Japan (Continental and Chineses)
- Morels
- White truffle
- Black truffle
- Summer truffle

FRUITS

Fruits and health are going hand by hand. Modern facilities for transport and storage allow a very wide choice and seasonal consumption all year long.

Not only refreshing but also fruits are stimulating appetite and are equally an important provider of vitamins and carbohydrates. Raw and not peeled they are producing more fibres.

In professional kitchens we are dividing fruits in the following categories:

Red fruits

- Strawberry
- Raspberry
- Grapes for wine or table
- Blackberry
- Mulberry
- Red currant
- White currant
- Gooseberry
- Etc.

Nuts

- Walnut
- Peanut
- Coconut
- Hazelnut
- Almond
- Pecan nut
- Pistachio
- Pinion
- Etc.

Piped fruits

- Apple
- Pear
- Quince
- Etc.

Stoned fruits

- Apricot

- Peach
- Prune
- Sherry
- Mirabelle plum
- Plum
- Nectarine
- Etc.

Exotic fruits

- Grapefruit
- Orange
- Lemon
- Lime
- Kumquat
- Sour orange
- Tangerine, etc.

Tropical fruits

- Banana
- Kiwi
- Fig
- Barbarie fig
- Granadina
- Mango
- Litchi
- Pineapple
- Guava
- Passion fruit
- Etc

Storage

Keep at about 5° centigrade, in a high humidity environment (85 to 90%),

How to keep them

- Refrigerated
- Frozen
- Sterilisation
- Cooking in sugar (jam)
- Cooking (marmalade)
- Drying

Common dried fruits

- Dried grape
- Fig
- Apricot
- Pear
- Apple
- Date
- Currant
- Prune
- Banana
- Etc.

Fruit products

In professional cooking we are using derivative product from fruits, such as

- Jam
- Marmalade
- Jelly

- Fruit nectarine
- Fruit juice
- Comfit
- Syrup
- Etc.

6. Spices and fine herbs, storage & humidity requirement

For a long time spices and fine herbs were considered a symbol of richness and power, and were even used as means of payment, today and thank to transport and storage facilities we dispose of a tremendous choice of spices from all over the world. Spices are coming from different sources such as seed, flower, leaf, root, etc. Today we find them fresh, frozen, dried, or kept in oil.

They are available grounded, all, granulated or preserved.

Everyday our chefs and cooks are using the power of spices and fine herbs to create new flavours and dishes, a well-spiced dish is a real art, in balance and creativity. We are doing a difference between using spices and spice mix.

Fresh, spices fine and herbs are bringing the most of flavours and colours to our dishes. All year long fine herbs are available in our markets, and are now a day an indispensable element in creative, regional and ethnic cooking.

Storage

Always keep spices and dried fine herbs hermetically closed in containers, away from humidity and ventilation. Order little quantity as, a long storage is affecting spices' aroma.

6. Food of animal origin, storage & humidity requirement

MILK AND MILK PRODUCT

By milk, it is understood, complete milk from healthy cows with the same grade of quality. Milk from other species, such as goat or sheep should be labeled as such.

100 g of milk are containing (average)

3.2 grams proteins
4.9 grams milk sugar (lactose)
3.7 grams milk fat
0.8 grams vitamins, mineral salts, oligo-elements
87.4 grams water

Storage

Milk is an easily altered product and is extremely sensible to other odours. It is necessary to keep it in special containers (glass, stainless steel, aluminium, Chinaware, porcelain), between 1 and 3° centigrade.

Different kinds of milk

Pasteurized milk

Whole milk, ready to drink and poor in germs. Louis Pasteur and his wife developed pasteurisation process around 1865.

The process is basically to bring milk briefly at 75° centigrade for 15 seconds, and cool it immediately. Stored in a cool area, pasteurized milk can be kept for about 10 days.

UHT-Milk (Ultra High Temperature)

Sterilized milk ready to drink. "Uperisation" process is sterilizing milk, and was created and patented in Switzerland. Milk is heated extremely fast to 130-150° centigrade, and immediately cooled at minus 5° centigrade and packed. Without refrigeration and hermetically closed UHT milk can be kept 11 weeks, but its taste then, will be slightly altered.

Skimmed milk

Whole milk partially skimmed with a 1.8% fat content. Can be made apt for conservation by pasteurisation or UHT process.

Lean milk

Whole milk partially or totally skimmed. With a maximum of 0.5% fat content. Can be made apt for conservation by pasteurisation or UHT process.

Mixed milk drinks

Drinks mixed with whole milk, partially skimmed or lean, prepared with ingredient brining flavours and different aromas. They are better known as milk shakes.

Concentrated milk

Whole milk sugared or not, where water was taken out by heat, in vacuum conditions (no air). Non sugared concentrated milk is always sterilised, sugared one is pasteurized or treated with the UHT process. Non sugared concentrated milk can be kept for one year, without refrigeration. Sugared one can be kept for two years.

Powdered milk

Whole milk powdered by pulverisation. This way it conserves its nutritive and energetic quality. Can be kept one year without refrigeration.

Cream

The centrifugation process of whole milk obtains cream. For general sales in markets, cream is treated exactly as the sterilised milk. This way can augment considerably conservation time, without alteration in taste.

Sorts of cream and fat content in percentage

Double cream	45%
Whole cream/to whip	35%
Half cream	25%

Acidulated cream 35%

Acidulated half cream 15%

BUTTER

To produce one kilogram of butter it is necessary to process 25 litres of milk (controlled for purity and quality) or 2.5 litres of cream.

Cream is beaten in a special container for butter (baratte) the same way as you would do with whipped cream, until flakes of butter will separate form milk.

Milk is then drained from butter flakes. Butter flakes are washed in iced water and brought back to the special butter container and processed until obtaining a malleable butter.

Storage

Always keep milk and milk products in the refrigerator between 1-3°centigrade, away

from light and odours. Butter can be kept 5 months in the refrigerator.

CHEESES

Gourmets and connoisseurs insist that a plate of cheese is the complement of a poor meal and crown a high one.

France, England, Germany, Switzerland, Italy and Holland are renowned around the world for the quality of their traditional cheeses.

We obtain cheese by coagulating milk with acids. Milk is coming from different animals such as cow, lamas, sheep, goat, buffalo, camel, etc.

Cheese is rich in nutritive elements such,

- Fat
- Albumin (proteins)
- Water

- Mineral salts
- Vitamins (B and especially, A, D, E, K, and carotene)

Storage

Keep away from light, air and heat.

Store at 4-12° centigrade with a maximum humidity factor of 80 to 90%. It is convenient to keep each cheese in adequate wrapping, to avoid a change and a mix of odours.

Take only wrapped cheese off the refrigerator half and hour before consumption, to let it recuperate its full aroma. The specialists call this process "chamber".

Fresh cheeses are to be the exception and are always serve cool from refrigeration.

Appreciated swiss cheeses

- Gruyere
- Emmental
- Sbrinz
- Tete de moine
- Fromage rabote
- Appenzellois
- Camembert Suisse
- Vacherin Fribourgeois
- Brie Suisse
- Tome Vaudoise
- Schabzieger Glaronais
- Reblochon
- Formaggini

EGGS

What was first? Egg or hen?

Following classification is in effect in Switzerland.

Extra class

Packing date, maximum 5 days after laying

Selling date, maximum 17 days after laying

A Class

Packing date, until 8 weeks after laying

Selling date, maximum 18 days after packing

B Class

Packing date, as A class

Selling date, no specification

C class

All eggs not corresponding to preceding prescription.

They will be used for industrial purposes and will be pasteurized

Imported eggs will have to bear the "IMP" label or the country of origin.

Size and class

- Small size	less than	50 grams
- Regular size	from	50 to 65 grams
- Big size	more than	65 grams

Eggs composition

One egg is composed of

- Shell
- Membrane
- White

- Yolk
- Germ
- Air chamber

Egg as a source of energy

- 100 grams of egg about 650 kj/155 kcal
- 100 grams of yolk about 1460 kj/ 350 kcal
- 100 grams of white about 230 kj/ 55 kcal

Storage

Store eggs in a dry and cool environment, away from heat and sun. Store at 1-2° centigrade.

Few ways to check eggs' freshness,

- **Taste test**: When breaking eggs, they should not have a rotten odour or smell kike hay.
- **Shaking test**: When egg is at its full freshness condition, shaking produces no sound.
- **Lighting test**: Non-fresh eggs feature stain and dark spots
- **Water test**: Dilute 100 grams of salt in a litre of water. Fresh eggs are staying at the bottom, meanwhile older eggs are floating.
- **View test**: Fresh eggs are featuring a round yolk, and white is firm and all.

Older eggs are spreading out on plate.

Few ways of conservation

- Refrigeration at 1-2° centigrade and around 90% air humidity
- Freezing at -045°centrigrade and store between -25 and -22°centigrade
- Pasteurizing

- Dehydrating by pulverisation
  - To obtain 1 litre of all eggs use about 25 normal size eggs
  - To obtain 1 litre of egg white use about 34 normal size eggs
  - To obtain 1 litre of egg yolk use about 44 normal size eggs

FAT AND COMESTIBLE OIL

When a fat substance is fluid at room temperature it is called oil, if it is compact it is called fat. Oils and fats are classified as follow:

1. Fats and animal origin oils

Obtained by pressure such as,

- Milk fats such as butter
- Fat from animal such as lard, fish oil, etc

2. Fats and vegetal oils

Obtained by fusion

- Fats from fruits such as olives, palm, etc.
- Fats from seeds such as peanut, sunflower, etc.

3. Legal disposition

All comestible fats bearing the name of a determined prime substance (i.e. pork fat, coconut oil) must be exclusively composed of it. Mixing fats and oils from different substances must be designed as cooking or frying oil, apt to consumption. Comestible fats bearing the mention "with butter" must have at least a 10% content of butter. All comestible oils bearing the name of a determined prime substance (i.e. olive oil, peanut oil) must be exclusively composed of it.

Artificial colouring is authorized.

Margarine

Margarine are processed industrially with vegetal or animal fats.

Storage

Keep fats and oils in fresh places away from light and air.

6

Basic Preparation Methods

The choice of basic cooking preparation is not a problem for who knows its merchandises and ingredients. For example: a piece of veal's hough can be roasted or boiled, but never pan-fried or grilled.

In the kitchen there is basically fourteen methods of preparation;

- Blanching
- Poaching
- Boiling
- Steam cooking
- Frying
- Pan frying (fast)
- Grilling
- Gratinating
- Oven cooking
- Roasting
- Braising
- Glazing
- Pan sweating
- Sweating

Due to constant technical progresses each professional should always be in tough with the new trends.

To cook food we have to transmit heat through:

- Water at a temperature between 65 to 100° centigrade
- Steam at a temperature between 100° to 120° centigrade
- Hot air at a temperature reaching until 280°centigrade
- Fat (frying) at a temperature between 130°C between 130° to 180°centigrade.
- Little fat (pan-frying) at a temperature reaching 180°centigrade.

BLANCHING

Short pre-cooking for divers reasons

- Take off heavy flavour of certain vegetables
- Take off bone's impurity
- Shortening cooking time

How to blanch?

- Blanch foodstuff in salted boiling water
- Blanch foodstuff in cold or hot water at the beginning of cooking process
- Blanch in frying oil at a temperature of about 130° centigrade
- Blanch by steaming or sweating with steam

Poaching

A soft preparation (temperature between 65° and 80° centigrade). Only tender aliment should be treated this way.

How to poach?

- In little liquid (wine or stock)
- In a lot of liquid (stock or water)

- In the Bain Marie, stirring (béarnaise)
- In the Bain Marie, not stirring
- In the new steaming device with temperature adjusting

BOILING

Cooking under boiling point (i.e. meat) or to boiling point (i.e. pastas)

How to boil?

- Just under boiling point
- Under boiling point
- Starting with cold liquid
- Starting with hot liquid
- Covered
- Uncovered

STEAM COOKING

Technical progress had tremendously influenced this type of cooking. Actually we can chose between cooking pot and inside grill, as used by our grand mothers, or the new pressure steamer, combo-steamer, or pressure cooker for large quantity.

How to cook with steam?

- With pressure
- Without pressure
- With water steam
- With dry steam
- Vacuum

FRYING

To fry, use only fats and oils with high combustion point

- Fry only small and dry quantities

- Fro frying breaded aliment in flower, egg or frying dough-shake excess.
- Always drain fat or oil excess from food-never cover

How to fry?

- At constant temperature
- Augmenting temperature
- Direct cooking (small food pieces)
- Pre-cooking at about 30°C (bigger pieces)

Pan frying

Only for food item with delicate fibres (meat marble), smaller or tender structures.

How to pan-fry?

- In a little pre-heated fat
- In a pan
- In a casserole
- On the grill

GRILLING

Take particular attention to heat level adequate to each piece!

Bigger piece of meat -fast and high intensity grilling and sizzling.

When pores are closed, it is recommended to slow down heat intensity, to allow cooking to the core of the piece.

How to grill?

Grill directly marinated food item.

- On charcoal grill
- On electric grill

- On gas grill
- In a pan grill

GRATINATING

Higher temperature needed (about 280°C). For few aliment (fine slices of fish, fine slices of vegetable) it will be the complete cooking process, otherwise pre-cook.

To obtain a nice colour and a round flavour, we are using the following ingredients: cheese, breadcrumb, crème, Sauce Hollandaise) sugar (for desserts).

How to gratinate?

- Under salamander at high temperature
- In the oven at high temperature from the top

OVEN COOKING

To cook in the oven it is not necessary to add fat or liquid (except sometimes for cooking trays, which will facilitate removing food item). Only dry heat will influence cooking.

How to oven cook?

- Conventionally in the oven, on a plaque, directly on the grill or in mould (glass, metal or earthenware)
- In hot air pulsated oven, on special plaques
- In steam combo-cooker

ROASTING

To start with, always at high temperature to form a crust and seal pores. Continue roasting at lower temperature, basting constantly with fat.

Attention: a) do not add liquid ruing roasting. B) Let the roast repose at least 20 minutes, before slicing.

How to roast?

- On a spit, basting constantly with fat
- In the oven, basting few times
- In hot air oven, basting few times

BRAISING

Braising is one of the most delicate preparation method. Meats pieces poor in fat will be "larded" before braising to keep aroma and taste. Braising is convenient for red meat, fish, vegetable and poultry. White meat and poultry will be glazed (see glazing). All braised items will be "wetted" to ¼ or 1/3 of its height and cooked in the oven, covered.

How to braise?

- First sizzle well red meat (to close pores), add vegetable or tomatoes or wet with red wine. Cover the piece until ¼ of its height with stock, cook in oven-wetting often- Cover.
- For fish use a "matignon". Then put the fish on a buttered holed tray (that will allow better handling of cooked fish). We will "wet" the fish with white wine and fish stock to a maximum of 1/3 of its height. Cook in the oven, covered, and "wetting" constantly.
- For vegetable (Belgium endive, fennel, etc) use a "matignon" or onions, or lard (i.e. for red cabbage) lay vegetable on top (sometime blanched) "wet" to 1/3 of white veal stock and cook in the oven, covered.
- For white and clear vegetable it is recommended to cover with buttered parchment paper or wax paper to avoid colour alteration.

GLAZING

We can glaze vegetables, poultry or white meat.

How to glaze?

- Sizzle well white meat and poultry, roasting at the same time a "morepoix", deglaze with white wine and "wet" with according stock until 1/6 of its height. Cook covered in the oven, "wetting" often. Before the end of the cooking process, take off cover and "wet" with reduced stock. That will give a glaze to the food item, thus the name "glazed".
- Vegetable will be first steamed, then glazed at the end of cooking process with a mix of juice and reduced adequate stock.

PAN SWEATING (POELER)

Pan sweating is a combination between sweating and roasting. For this characteristic, only soft and tender piece of meat will be processed this way. Cooking will start covered, in the oven at a temperature of about 150°C. At the end of cooking process, temperature will be brought at about 180°C, cover will be taken away. That will give the piece of meat its nice brownish colour.

How to pan sweat?

- With little fat and no other liquid, covered in the oven at a 150°C to start, wetting constantly with its own juice. Take off cover at the end of cooking process and bring temperature to 180°C, to give the piece of meat its brownish colour.

SWEATING

For vegetables, meat and mushroom.

How to sweat?

- Mix the ingredient to sweat with fat substance, if necessary onion (goulash) and other vegetables. Add adequate liquid (Stock, wine) and sweat slowly in a covered pan.

- Use lonely adequate recipients with adequate covers.

Most usual cooking methods in assembly kitchens

1. Steam cooking and steam cooking with or without pressure
2. Vacuum pack cooking
3. Low temperature roasting
4. Pan frying
5. Grilling
6. Poaching
7. Regeneration cooking (bring back to temperature)

Most common equipment and machinery used in assembly kitchen

To realize assembly kitchen in optimal conditions, it is necessary to associate intermediary product and new techniques and cooking methods.

- Convention oven
- Steamer/auto-cooker/jet-cooker (with or without pressure)
- Combo-cooker
- Microwave oven
- Salamander
- Induction stove
- Shock freezer (blast)
- Electronic scale
- Vacuum pack machine

STEAMER

Have few names according to countries: Auto-cooker high performance, pressure cooker, jet-cooker or fast cooker.

Among the fourteen fundamental and known ways to prepare foods, four can be processes in the steamer.

- Blanching

- Poaching
- Boiling
- Steaming

Steam cooking is one of the most ancient methods. Chinese are using this method for more than 4000 years. Mr. Pappin, a Yugoslav scientist, invented the first steamer with pressure in 1681.

The steam that we are using for cooking is water that is transformed for a liquid state to a gaseous state. Pure steam is invisible. Steam becomes visible when it is condensing partially, which means that it is becoming water again. Steam that you can observe above a casserole is then a mix of air and water drop.

Steam is an excellent heat vector. Its volume is approximately 1000 times superior to water. One deciliter of water gives about 100 litres of steam. It is then much more economical to cook with steam than cook with water.

Beside, water can only reach a maximal temperature of 100°centigrade.

Temperature of water steam depends on the pressure. When water is heated in a closed and sealed container, it produces steam. The more the pressure augments in this container, the more the temperature is elevating, such elevated temperature is shortening cooking time. It is not the pressure, which permits to cook faster, but the highest temperature.

The measure unit to determine the pressure of the steam water in a steamer is called the bar. One bar corresponds to about 120° centigrade.

We can represent the relation between pressure and temperature with the following mean:

- Steam is produced in a steam generator or with the help of separated water boiler to be further injected directly in the cooking container, on the food items. Food items are inserted preferably on holed "Gastronorm". It is exclusively the pressure process that allows the saturated steam to reach high temperature, without loosing its humidity. That is reducing considerably cooking time for vegetables, potatoes, cereals, etc. It has also the advantage of keeping the colours of difficult vegetables such as beans and cauliflower.

COMBO-STEAMERS/AEROSTEAMER

Recognized also, as hot air steam cooker, combined steam cooker, etc.

As its name is indicating this device is a multifunctional machine. It is in fact an improvement of the air convection oven. It works with two fluids, hot air and steam, that can be used separately, simultaneously or one after the other one.

In the "hot air" mode, with or without steaming, between 40 to 250°Centigrade, this device permits,

- Oven cooking
- Roasting, low temperature roasting
- Braising, stewing
- Gratinating, mixed cooking
- Regeneration.

The mix steam-oxygen is uniformly distributed in the cooking device by ventilation. Cooking times are superior to steam cookers. More than 200 cooking process can be added to the machine's memory.

The processor is watching automatically the desired cooking style, cooking temperature, external temperature and time.

MICROWAVE

The central head of each microwave is the magnetron. That is where the electromagnetic waves or microwaves are produced.

They are sent in the cooking chamber by a distributor to allow the repartition on food items. Water molecules in food items are brought by microwaves to oscillate strongly.

The .....heat produced by friction is warming the food items. Since the microwaves are reflected by metal, never use plates or trays with metal content in the microwave oven. International studies have proved that microwave oven used correctly have no negative incidence on food.

INDUCTION STOVES

Utilization of induction stoves is identical to regular stove. An electronic generator produces a magnetic camp that gives energy exactly where needed. When a ferromagnetic bottom pan is placed in the magnetic camp, whirling currents will appear at he pan's bottom. This process will produce heating current in the pan's bottom and thus a heating of the contents. Cooking surface is vitro-ceramic and not magnetic. It will produce no heat on itself.

The energy is released immediately and adjusted very precisely, heat is produced as soon as the pan is on the cooking surface, and disappears immediately when the pan is removed.

This device has a high thermal strength (about 85°C) and minimal heat radiance, which reduce energy consumption and protect environment. To cook on induction a special cooking battery is needed.

VITRO-CERAMIC COOKING SURFACES OR GRIDDLE

The cooking or roasting surface in this device is an ultra hard and solid vitro-ceramic sheet. It is extremely resistant to heat variation. An infrared heater produced the temperature that comes to food through the vitro-ceramic. The (little) thickness of the sheet allows fast heating and good temperature's regulation. This device is of low consumption. Most of the hose devices are equipped with an automatic detection that regulates energy only when food is on the sheet.

Aliments are dropped directly on the sheet. This non-porous surface does need a minimum of fat.

SEQUENTIAL BURNER

Most of food preparations demand a steady temperature in cooking container. Studies have shown that this result can be obtained also when heat is not provided continuously but periodically. That is why, a system was created that is controlling the arrival of gas to the burner and open it periodically (one period = one service time/a dead time, during about 40 seconds). Burner can be programmed to heat rapidly with a strong flame or slowly with a low flame, continuously or periodically.

The gas pipe bringing gas to the open burner is supplied with a security valve that assures also the alimentation of gas for the ignition flame. A heat regulator also manages the security valve.

Beside that, the security valve that manages the periodical alimentation in gas can also be controlled with a manual regulator. Which means that even in case of electricity shortening, work can continue, as with a regular stove.

7

Mastering the Food and Beverage Cycle

OPERATION MANAGEMENT I

The neglected sub-systems that drain profits:

- Purchasing
- Receiving
- Storage
- Issuing, controls

The importance of purchasing, receiving and storage for the restaurant's bottom line are explored in depth. The use of purchase specifications is stressed and a discussion of the different purchasing methods is held. An introduction to federal quality and yield grading is given and the supplier selection process is reviewed.

The role of the receiving clerk and the set-up of the receiving area are discussed. The flow of product and paperwork from receiving through storage is traces with reference to control implications.

Inventory tracking methods are introduced and correct storage procedures are reviewed.

Readings:

- Product specification sheet
- Cover letter
- Receiving
- Skills required by the receiving clerk
- Storage
- Forms used in purchasing, receiving, storage and issuing

PRODUCT SPECIFICATION SHEET

Product : ____________________

Grade : ____________________

Trim factor : ____________________

Weight range : ____________________

Method of tenderisation : ____________________

____

____

Packaging : ____________________

Special consideration : ____________________

____

____

____

State of refrigeration : ____________________

____

SAMPLE COVER LETTER TO BE SENT TO PURVEYORS

To

XYZ Meat Packing Company

Beautiful road

New Delhi

Gentlemen,

We are happy to inform you that you have been selected as a potential source of supply four our hotel/ restaurant facility. In order for both of our businesses to prosper, we must develop a good working relationship, this cover letter, attached to our specifications is sent to you as a first step towards developing good business relations.

All meats, primal, wholesale, cuts, portions cuts, variety meats, processed or unprepared items shall be purchased through USDA (or whatever specification your country is using) inspected purveyors only. Beef, lamb, and veal shall be graded Prime or Choice by an USDA official and no other grades will be received.

All merchandise shall be in excellent condition when delivered and must conform to our specifications. All items shall meet the requirement of weight range, grade, condition, and quality at all times. Tolerances will be limited to adverse market conditions and only with our prior approval.

All products will be closely examined upon delivery. Tare weights will be determined for each product and only net weights will be accepted rather than any printed weights on the packaging material. All other aspect of the specifications will be strictly enforced at all times and it is required that the purveyor cooperate to the fullest in preparing and shipping products for acceptance.

All products shall be in sanitary condition, free form undesirable odours, blood clots, bruises, discoloration or other blemishes. In situations where such defects are found concealed within the product, the purveyor will be expected to make adjustments even after the product have been accepted.

Any product ordered in the fresh state shall be in excellent condition, possessing the quality, odour, colour, and other attributed typical of that grade and cut of meat. Items called for in the frozen state shall show no evidence of thawing and shall be packaged properly to prevent freezer burn. If for just cause, such as late delivery, lack of staff, or other such emergency conditions, a shipment of products is accepted without thorough inspection and found to be undesirable later, the purveyor will be expected to pick up the items on his next scheduled delivery date.

Should you have any questions concerning these policies and procedures, please contact our Food and Beverage Director, Mr. XYZ.

Sincerely,

RECEIVING

Introduction

Receiving is a key control point in a Food and Beverage operation. When functioning p.operly, its checks and balances make the purchasing department accountable for its actions (or lack of action). Merchandise is money and it is as important to be assured of every penny at the receiving dock as it is to balance the cash bank in the registers. Failure at either will produce the same results.

Financial Loss

Functions of the receiving department.

1. Insures product quality, quantity and condition.
2. Aids purchasing department in evaluation of suppliers performance.
3. Functions as control points or checks on the purchasing agent.
4. Acts as an accounting checkpoint, providing a verified invoice to compare to billing statements.
5. Maintains product condition by minimising time that items are delayed form going into production or storage.
6. Informs purchasing and production of shortages resulting from incomplete deliveries or returns.

Skills required by the receiving clerk

1. Knowledge of product characteristics.
2. Knowledge of product quality.
3. Knowledge of product weight ranges.
4. Knowledge of product trim factors.
5. Knowledge of acceptable product condition.
6. Knowledge of proper packaging material.

Storage

1. What is the purpose of storage?

A. Protects merchandise from loss through theft or spoilage.

B. Supply operation with its needs, in amount needed and where it is needed.

2. Who is responsible for storage?

A. Controller

- Accountability
- Supervise system
- Inventories

B. Storeroom Manager

- Daily operation
- Personnel
- Sanitation
- Security
- Implement control
- Records
- Delivery set-up

3. What storeroom equipment is needed to operate?

- Shelves (18" – 20" deep, 16" – 18" high)
- Pallets or dunnage racks
- Electric- motorised truck
- Two-decked delivery truck
- Flat bed truck
- Scales: floor, table, and portion
- Wall cabinets for valuables
- Uniforms, freezer coats

4. What are the storage areas?

A. Dry

- Dry foods
- Liquor
- Mineral water
- Cleaning supplies
- Pots, pans, chinaware, flatware, glassware, hollowware, etc.
- Paper and plastics
- Accounting supplies

B. Refrigerated

- Fresh meat, poultry, fruits, vegetables, and dairy products
- Fish box

- Smoked meats box
- Delicatessen box
- Wine
- Beer/soft drinks: draft and bottle

C. Freezer

- Meats, fish, vegetables, seafood, poultry

D. Commissary

- Butcher Shop
- Salad & vegetable preparation

D. Ingredient Room

E. Satellite Storage

F. Garbage and trash

G. Bonded goods

5. How can theft be prevented?

A. Personnel Screening

B. Secure areas

C. Adequate, strong locks

D. Key Control Systems

- Limited authorization
- Attach to personal key ring
- Available to limited number of people
- Do not issue to front desk or Engineer on permanent basis
- Maintain emergency keys in sealed & signed envelopes

E. Staff on duty when storeroom is open, or doors are unlocked

6. What are the recommended storage practices for the prevention of spoilage?

A. Wine storage

Recommended practices for wine storage

1. Store bottles on side or cases upside down
2. Temperature: generally 50°-55° F.
3. Separate wines into: Red, white, rose, sparkling, champagne and fortified
4. Avoid excessive light, temperature, dampness, movement that may affect wine.

B. Dry storage

Recommended practices for dry storage

1. Store products off floor on clean surfaces to permit cleaning floor areas and to protect from contamination.
2. Do not store products under exposed sewer or water lines or next to sweating walls
3. Store all poisonous materials, including pesticides, soap and detergents away from food supplies
4. Keep shelving and floor clean and dry at all times.
5. Schedule cleaning of storage area at regular intervals
6. Date all merchandise upon receipt and rotate on a "first in – first out" basis
7. Locate most frequently needed items on lower shelves and near entrance
8. Store heavy packages on lower shelves

C. Refrigerated storage

Recommended practices for refrigerated storage

1. All cooked food or other products removed form original container must be enclosed in clean, sanitized, covered, containers and be properly labeled
2. Do not store packaged food in contact with water or undrained ice
3. Check refrigerator thermometer regularly

- Produce 45°F (7°C) or below

- Dairy/Meat 40°F (4°C) or below
- Seafood 30°F (-1°C) or below

4. Store large pieces of meat and all foods to permit free circulation of cool air on all surfaces
5. Do not store food directly on floor or base
6. Schedule cleaning of equipment and refrigerated storage rooms at regular intervals
7. Date all merchandise upon receipt and rotate inventory on a "first in- first out" basis
8. Check fruits and vegetables daily for spoilage
9. Store dairy products separately form strong odoured foods. Store fish apart form other food products
10. Establish preventive maintenance program for equipment

D. Freezer storage

Recommended practices for frozen storage

1. Promptly store frozen foods at 0°F (-18°) or below
2. Check freezer thermometer frequently
3. Cover all food containers
4. Defrost as necessary to eliminate excessive frost build-up. If practical, defrost when the least a mount of food is in storage
5. Plan your opening of the freezer. Get what you need at one time to reduce the loss of cold air
6. Remove contents to another freezer when defrosting to permit thorough cleaning and to keep contents dry.
7. Date all merchandise upon receipt and rotate inventory on a "first in – first out" basis
8. Keep shelving and floor clean at all times
9. Establish preventive maintenance program for equipment

SAMPLE OF RECEIVING CLERK'S DAILY REPORT

RECEIVING CLERK'S DAILY REPORT

– – – –

Date: – – – – Clerk's Name: – – – – – –

Item	Quantity	Unit	Unit Price	Supplier	Invoice	Total amount	Distribution		Sundries
							Production	Storage	

SAMPLE OF MEAT STORAGE TAG

To be attached with each food items entering storage facilities

#:	10946			#:	10946		
Date received:	sep-21	Date received:	sep-21				
Item:	Striploin	Grade:	Prime	Item:	Striploin	Grade:	Prime
Weight:	12LBS	@	3.00	Weight:	12 LBS	@	3.00
Purveyor:	Cross	Extension:	$ 36.00	Purveyor:	Cross	Extension:	$ 36.00
Issue by:	Oct.6	Issue by:	Oct. 6				
Date issued:	Oct. 1	Date issued:	Oct.1				
				Issued to:			
				Main			
				Kitchen			

OPERATION MANAGEMENT II

Beverage Management, the Wine List, Food and Wine

The wine list structure and format is explained. The size and extent of the wine list is discussed and a review is made of the principal wine-growing regions of the world. The importance of wine and liquor sales as profit - makers is stressed and the promotion of wine in the restaurant is discussed. Finally, wine-pricing methods are analysed.

Readings

Wine list development

Pricing policies for wine

WINE LIST DEVELOPMENT

Market Considerations

A. The type of restaurant - Fine dining, Bistro, Family, etc.

B. Clientele

   1. Income (price sensitivity)
   2. Wine knowledge
   3. Dining occasion
   4. How the check is paid (cash, credit card, and corporate account)

C. Competitors wine offerings.

Operational factors

A. Storage Space

B. Capital tied up in inventory

C. Controls

D. Long terms- future purchasing vs. Week to week buying

Menu compatibility

A. Style of cuisine

B. Complexity

C. Price range compatibility

D. Seasonability considered

Selecting wine for the list

A. Blind tasting

1. By region
2. By grape variety
3. By cost
4. Final selections paired with menu items

Breath vs. depth of the wine list

A. Consider the menu

B. Location. Are you near a wine region?

C. Length of the list

D. Should we specialize?

E. Should we balance the list by country and by region

Other considerations

A. Name brands that have special appeal

B. Celebration wines

C. Value wines from lesser-known producers

A model for an international list for a 125- seat restaurant

A. 60 wines

B. Initial inventory – 500 to 600 bottles

C. Initial investment - $ 6,000 to & 8,000

D. Suggested structure of list
   1. Sparkling wine and Champagne
      a) 3 French (1 prestige cuvee)
      b) 2 American
      c) 1 Spanish
   2. White wines
      a) 12 American
      b) 10 French
      c) 4 Australian
      d) 4 Italian
      e) 3 German
   3. Red wines
      a) 8 American
      b) 8 French
      c) 3 Italian
      d) 2 Spanish

VIII. Pricing strategy

A. Fixed mark-up
B. Mark-up plus handling cost
C. Progressive pricing
D. Contribution margin pricing
E. Fixed priced wine list

IX. Tracking sales and revising the list

A. 80/20 rule
B. Wine list engineering

X. Staff training

A. Tasting on regular basis

B. References and resources
C. Food and wine sessions
D. Video and role playing
E. Incentives

XI. Wine promotion

A. Wine by the glass program
B. Tasting portions
C. Wine and food dinners
D. Wine classes
E. Winemaker presentations at luncheon or dinner
F. Special fixed priced sinners, which include wine

FEW PRICING STRATEGY

Fixed Markup

1.

Cost	X	Markup	=	Selling Price
6	X	3	=	18
12	X	3	=	36
20	X	3	=	60
30	X	3	=	90

2.

Cost	+	CM + Handling			=	Selling Price
6	+	10	+	3	=	19
12	+	10	+	3	=	25
20	+	12	+	5	=	37
30	+	15	+	6	=	51

Regressive Markup

3.

Cost	X	Markup	=	Selling Price	Gross Profit
6	X	3	(33%) =	18	12
12	X	2.5	(40%) =	30	18
20	X	2	(50%) =	40	20
30	X	1.75	(57%) =	52	22

RATING BEVERAGE SERVICE

- Appropriate Glassware and Equipment
- The service staff's knowledge of beverages offered

TECHNICAL EXPERTISE

- Product served at the appropriate time
- Product served at the appropriate temperature
- Wine bottle presented and opened correctly
- Wine decanted correctly if needed
- Wine poured correctly and to the appropriate level
- Glasses refilled as needed
- Empty glasses removed from table quickly
- New glasses brought to table if additional wine is ordered.

THINGS TO CONSIDER WHEN RARING THE WINE LIST

1. Is it clean, attractive and easy to read?
2. Does it fit the personality of the restaurant?
3. Is it comparable with the menu offerings?
4. Is it customer oriented or just an ego-trip?

5. Is it user friendly (Staff & customers)?
6. Does it provide the correct information in the correct format with the correct spelling?
7. Are the vintages listed and are they correct?
8. Are the wines in stock or just on the list to win awards?
9. Does the service staff know the list?
10. Are the prices reasonable for the wines and the operation?

8

Practical Cooking

A) DEMONSTRATION ON STOCKS

WHITE STOCK

Ingredients	Qty
Chicken bones	500 g
Carrots	50 g
Onions	30 g
Celery	10 g
Parsley stalk	3-5 nos
Bayleaf	2 nos
Pepper corn	6 nos
Cloves	2-3 nos
Water	1.5 lit

Method

1) Cut bones in large pieces and rinse them in cold water.
2) Wash and place the bones into a stock-pot and add cold water.
3) Bring to a boil and skim out the scum, add vegetables.

4) Allow the stock to simmer for at least 2 hrs. At this time the fat will rise up to the surface during this time the fat should be constantly skimmed.

5) Pass through a muslin cloth and reboil and place aside to cool.

BROWN STOCK/VEAL STOCK/MUTTON STOCK (FOND BRUN OR FOND ESTOUFFADE)

Ingredients	Qty
Beef/veal/mutton bones	500 g
Carrots	40 g
Onions	25 g
Bouquet garni	
Celery	12 g
Parsley stalk	6 g
Bay leaf	½ no
Thyme	½ spring
Beef fat or any other fat	A little to brown the bones

Method

1) Cut or break the bones in 3-4 pieces and place it into a roasting tray with fat or oil.

2) Roast the trimmings until rich brown in a hot oven, place in a stock pot.

3) Cover with water, bring to boil and skim.

WHITE FISH STOCK (FOND DE POISSON BLANC)

Ingredients	Qty
Butter	15 g
Finely sliced onions	50 g
Bay leaf	1 no

Peppercorns	2-3 nos
Parsley stalk	4 g
Fish bones and trimmings (surmai or rahu)	400 g
White mushrooms	3 g
Lemon juice	¼ lime
Cold water	1 lit

Method

1) Place the aromatic in the bottom of a buttered saucepan on top the blanched shredded onions.
2) Add the cleaned and cut fish bones and trimmings.
3) Add in the lemon juice and sweat the bones etc. place onto a grease-proof paper.
4) Moisten with eater, bring to a boil, skim, allow to simmer for 20 mins.
5) Strain to a muslin cloth, reboil and cool or use as required.

Vegetable stock is prepared as the same way as white fish stock only the chicken is replaced by vegetables (carrots, turnips, French beans etc can be used) but veg stock should be kept at least for half an hour.

B) SAUCES

BECHAMEL SAUCE OR WHITE SAUCE

Ingredients	Qty
Flour	90 g
Butter	90 g
Milk	1 lit
Onion studded with clove and bayleaf	25 g

Method

1) Bring the milk to a boil with the studded onion and bring to a boil.

2) Melt the butter in a thick bottom pan.

3) Add the flour, stir and cook the roux over a gentle fire without colouring till it gets a sandy texture. Pour the milk into the roux stirring with a wooden spoon to avoid lumps. Simmer gently for an hr. remove the studded onion and pass through a fine strainer, cover with butter to prevent the formation of skin.

VELOUTE SAUCE

Ingredients	Qty
Butter	90 g
Flour	90 g
Stock (chicken/veal/fish)	1 lit
Mushroom trimmings	25 g

Method

1) in a thick bottom pan, Prepare blond roux. (slightly brown)
2) add cold stock into the roux, stir vigorously to avoid lumps.
3) Add mushroom trimmings.
4) Simmer gently for an hour, stirring frequently with a wooden spoon.
5) Pass through a fine strainer and cover with butter to prevent the formation of skin.

Note: fish veloute should be cooked for 20 mins only and white wine should be added at a latter stage.

BROWN SAUCE OR ESPAGNOLE SAUCE

Ingredient	Qty
Fat	60 g
Flour	70
Tomato puree	30 g

Brown stock	1.5 lit
Fat	15 g
Carrots grated	70 g
Onions chopped	70 g
Fresh pork rind finely chopped	10 g
Parsley, celery, bay leaf	3 g

Method

1) Prepare brown roux in a heavy bottom pan and cool.
2) Add tomato puree, stirring to prevent lumps.
3) Gradually mix in hot stock, stirring vigorously to blend well and cook on a gentle heat.
4) Sauté the mirepoix in fat and add the sautéed veg. to the sauce.
5) Simmer gently for 4-6 hrs.
6) Remove the scum when it comes to the top.
7) Strain and cover with a thin layer of butter.

Note: overbrowning should be avoided, as this tends to make the sauce taste bitter.

HOLLANDAISE SAUCE

Ingredient	Qty
Butter	200 g
Egg yolk	2 Nos
Crushed peppercorns	5 nos
Vinegar	15 ml
Lemon juice	½ nos

Method

1) Melt the butter in a pan and keep aside.

2) Place the crushed peppercorns and vinegar in a pan and reduce completely.
3) Add one tablespoon of water and cool.
4) Add the egg yolk and whisk.
5) Place the pan in a double boiler and whisk the egg yolk till a sabayon is formed (thickens). Then add in the melted butter until it is blended and forms a smooth sauce. Add lemon juice.
6) Strain through a fine strainer, correct the seasoning if reqd.
7) Store at 30-37°C if necessary.

Tomato sauce

Ingredient	Qty
Flour	80 g
Butter	70 g
Dices of bacon trimmings	40 g
Onions	80 g
Carrots grated	80 g
Celery	40 g
Bay leaf	1-2 nos
Garlic crushed	2 nos
Tomato puree	100 g
Tamato chopped	50 g
Brown stock	450 ml
Sugar	10 g
Salt	3 g

Method

1) Melt the butter in a pan
2) Add the roughly chopped veg. crushed garlic and sauté, tell slightly brown.

3) Mix the flour till it gets a sandy texture and gets a slightly brown colour.
4) Add in the tomato puree and chopped tomatoes and stir.
5) Add cold stock, stirring to prevent lump[s and bring to boil.
6) Add the seasoning and cook for 1½ hr.
7) Skim frequently.
8) Strain and cover with butter.

MAYONNAISE SAUCE

Ingredient	Qty
Salad oil or olive oil	1 lit
Egg yolk	8 nos
French mustard	¼ TSP
Vinegar	25 ml
Lemon juice	of 1 no
Seasoning	to taste

Method

1) Place yolks of eggs, vinegar, seasonings in a clean bowl and whisk well.
2) Add oil slowly, a little at a time, whisking continuously, until all the oil is incorporated.
3) Finish the sauce by adding the juice of lemon and warm water. This is done to ensure coherence of the sauce and to prevent it turning curdling, mayonnaise is suitable for serving with fish, meat and hors d'oeuvres.

D) DEMONSTRATION ON EGG COOKERY

POACHED EGG

Ingredient	Qty
Eggs	4 nos
Salt	As regd

Vinegar	5 ml
Water	Approx 1 lit

Method

1) Keep water to boil in a *degchi* with vinegar and salt.
2) Lower the flame till the water is simmering and break in one egg slowly. Do not let it spread out too much. Season with salt and pepper.
3) When the white coagulates remove the egg slowly.
4) Repeat it with the remainder of the eggs.

BOILED EGGS

Ingredient	Qty
Eggs	4 Nos
Salt	As Reqd
Vinegar	5 ml
Water	Approx 1 lit

Method

1) Boil the water with salt and vinegar.
2) For a quarter boiled egg put into the hot water for 15 seconds remove crack into a bowl/cup. Season with salt and pepper.
3) For a half boiled egg put it into the hot water for half a minute and repeat the above procedure.
4) For hard boiled egg leave the egg in the water for 10 mins remove, let it cool slightly and remove the shell and use as required.

SCRAMBLED EGG

Ingredient	Qty
Eggs	4 Nos

Milk	50 ml
Salt	as reqd
Butter	5 g

Method

1) Break the eggs in a pan, add the butter, salt and milk and whisk together.
2) Cook over a slow flame whisking all the time. Serve hot over a toast.
3) Serve hot.

FRIED EGGS

Ingredient	Qty
Eggs	8 nos
Oil	10 ml
Salt	as reqd
Pepper	as reqd

Method

1) Heat the oil in a pan when hot break the egg in and season.
2) Cook as reqd, either sunny side up or a double fried keeping the yolk firm.
3) Serve hot.

OMELETTE STUFFED WITH TOMATOES AND CELERY

Ingredient	Qty
Eggs	8 nos
Oil	50 ml
Salt	as reqd

Milk	50 ml
Pepper	as reqd
Tomatoes	2 nos
Celery	1 stem finely chopped
Coriander leaves	few spring

Method

1) Break 2 eggs in a bowl, add some milk and beat.
2) Heat oil in a pan, add the egg mixture in and scrambled slightly and let it set slightly.
3) Put in concasse tomatoes (boil water and add the tomatoes and when the skin comes out then peel remove the seeds and chop)
4) Add celery and coriander to the tomato. Season with salt and pepper.
5) Fold the omelette, and turn out on a plate.

OEUFS AND COCOTTE

Ingredient	Qty
Eggs	4 nos
Salt	As reqd
Butter	10 g

Method

1) Grease 4 cocotte moulds or use 4 small baba moulds.
2) Break an egg in each mould, season and put butter on it.
3) Fill a baking tray with water, lower the cocottes in the water and cover them. Cook in the oven till the egg whites coagulates.
4) Bake at required temperature and time.

BOILED RICE

Ingredient	Qty
Water	4-5 times the rice
Rice	500 g
Salt	as reqd

Method

1) Boil the water with salt and add a little oil. Pick wash and clean the rice and keep it aside.
2) When the water boils profusely add the washed rice.
3) Boil till the rice is just 3/4th done and strain in a colander and keep aside.
4) Use as required.

DAL TADKA

Ingredient	Qty
Tuvoor dal	200 g soak and keep aside
Oil	50 ml
Curry leaves	1 spring
Green chilles	2-3 nos chopped finely
Garlic	4-5 flakes
Whole red chilli	2 Nos for the tadka
Turmeric Pd	as reqd
Salt	as reqd
Onions	½ no finely chopped
Tomatoes	½ no sliced
Coriander leaves	few springs
Rye	2 g
Hing	1 g

Method

1) Pick wash and clean the dal soak in water for 10-15 mins.
2) In a dechi add the washed dal, turmeric powder green chilli, onions and boil it till the dal is mashed up completely, keep whisking.
3) Once done, keep all the ingredients ready for the tadka.
4) Heat oil in a pan, add the rye let it crackle then add the curry leaves, hing, whole red chilli, green chilli, garlic, etc.
5) Pour the tadka over the dal and finally garnish with coriander leaves.
6) Serve hot.

ALOO GOBI MASALA

Ingredient	Qty
Aloo	250 g
Cauliflower	150 g
Onions	1 No
Tomato	1 no small
Oil	50 ml
Curry leaves	2 springs
Coriander leaves	A few spring finely chopped
Hing	2 g
Red chilli powder	As reqd
Salt	as reqd
Garlic	3-4 nos
Mustard seeds (Rye)	2 g

Method

1) Boil the potatoes in water and cool peel the skin off and cut it into small cubes.

2) Cut the cauliflower into florets and keep them in salted water for 5-6 mins and then boil in the same water. Keep them aside.
3) Heat oil in a pan, add the hing flowed with curry leaves, rye, onions, garlic, green chillies, red chilli powder, tomatoes and fry the masala well, once done add in the potatoes an cauliflower and mix well.
4) Add salt, and mix well. Garnish with coriander leaves.
5) Serve hot along with dal and rice.

SEMIYA KHEER/PAYASAM

Ingredient	Qty
Milk	800 ml
Vermicelli	100 g
Mava	50 g
Cashewnuts	20 g
Ghee	20 ml
Sugar	100 g
Elaichi powder	a pinch

Method

1) Fry vermicelli till golden brown.
2) Reduce the milk with sugar till fairly thick, add the brown vermicelli and simmer.
3) When vermicelli is soft add the grated mava, roasted cashew nuts and elaichi powder.
4) Serve hot garnished with a few roasted cashew nuts.

MENU 2

CREAM OF TOMATO SOUP

Ingredient	Qty
Tomatoes	400 g
Carrots	50 g

Onions	100 g
Celery	1 stalk chopped
Stock/water	800 ml
Milk	200 ml
Refined flour	60 g
Salt	to taste
Pepper	to taste
Sugar	a little
Vinegar	2-5 ml
Oil	5 ml to fry
Butter	30 g
Bread	2 slices

Method

1) Chop up the onions tomato and celery and grate the carrots. Add the stock/water and boil the veg. till soft and well done, cool and puree.
2) Stain the puree. Keep aside.
3) Make a béchamel sauce and add the strained puree to it and simmer.
4) Cut the croutons of bread and deep fry them in oil till crisp.
5) Season the soup with salt and pepper, vinegar, sugar. Serve hot with garnish of fried bread croutons.

PULLET A LA REX

Ingredient	Qty
Chicken	1 no
Chicken stock	400 ml
Ref, flour	50 g
Mushrooms	115 g
Cream	55 g

Capsicum	55g
Egg yolk	2 nos
Parsley	few spring
Salt and pepper powder	to taste
Bread slice	4 nos
Butter	50 g

Method

1) Boil the chicken in water, when chicken is done, skin out and dice. Strain stock and reserve it.
2) Cut mushroom and capsicum, sauté them in little butter, remove them and keep aside.
3) Melt butter and flour and make a blond roux. Add the chicken stock, and finish off with cream and egg yolk laison. Season well.
4) Add in the diced chicken and the sautéed veg.
5) Fry the slices of bread to golden brown, and place the chicken mixture on the fried bread and garnish with chopped parsley and serve hot.

GLAZED CARROTS

Ingredient	*Qty*
Carrots 250 g	
Sugar	10 g
Butter	10 g
Salt	as reqd
Water	to cook the carrots

Method

1) Peel, wash and cut the carrots in payasannes shapes.

2) Melt butter add the carrots and toss. Adds salt, sugar and enough water to cook the carrots.
3) Serve and cook the carrots till done, but firm.
4) Serve hot as an accompaniment to the main course.

CARAMEL CUSTARD

Ingredient	Qty
Milk	250 ml
Eggs	2 nos
Vanilla essence	Few Drops
Sugar	60 g
Sugar for caramel	50 g
Nutmeg powder	a pinch

Method

1) Make a caramel out of the 50 g of sugar (light brown in colour by cooking it on flame) and line it in the moulds.
2) Mix 60 g sugar and eggs. Boil the milk bring it to room temp. and add in the egg and sugar mixture. Add vanilla essence and strain and then add nutmeg powder.
3) Line a large jelly mould or small individual moulds fill the moulds with the mixture and bake it in a tray filled with water into a preheated oven.
4) Bake at 150 c for approx 15-20 mins or till firm.
5) Once done cool completely and demould and serve.

MENU 3

FRENCH ONION SOUP

Ingredient	*Qty*
Onions	250 g
Butter	20 g

Oil	10 ml
Brown stock	1 lit
Bread slice	4 nos
Cheese	60 g
Garlic	2 g
Woshestireshire sauce	5 ml
Salt and pepper powder	to taste

Method

1) Slice onions finely. In a heavy saucepan, melt butter and oil and add the chopped onions and them till light golden.
2) Remove half the onions and continue frying rest of them till golden brown in colour and crisp.
3) To the initial lot of onions add brown stock and simmer for around 15 mins.
4) Add in the 2nd lot of onions, Wooster sauce, salt and pepper.
5) Cut the bread slices in large croutes, toast them till golden brown in colour, rub the garlic onto it and then put the grated cheese and toast again in the salamamder.
6) Serve the soup hot in a soup bowl and garnish it with the croute at the last minute.

HUNGARIAN GOULASH

Ingredient	Qty
Beef	500 g
Flour	30 g
Onions	100 g
Salt and pepper powder	to taste
Capsicum	50 g
Oil	30 ml

Tomatoes	100 g
Brown stock	½ lit
Bay leaf	2 nos
Paprika powder	2 g
Parsley	¼ bunch

Method

1) Clean and cut the beef into small even sized cubes and roll them in flour.
2) Chop onions and capsicum in hot oil, add the meat into it and sear well.
3) Blanch the tomato and concasse. Add the tomato into that meat and stock, bouquet garni. Simmer till the beef gets done.
4) Remove the bouquet garni season and serve hot.

POTATO ANNA

Ingredient	Qty
Potatoes	500 g
Butter	50 g
Salt and white pepper powder	to taste

Method

1) Peel wash and cut the potatoes into roundles, par boil and drain keep aside.
2) Grease a jelly mould, arrange a layer of potatoes, apply butter and season, repeat with more potatoes and arrange them in overlapping layers.
3) When the mould is full, press the potatoes lightly using another jelly mould.
4) Cook in a moderate oven for round 20 mins. (150° C to 180° c)

5) Remove and turn the mould over. Flash under the salamander if required to get a golden brown colour.
6) Serve hot as an accompaniment to the main course.

BREAD AND BUTTER PUDDING

Ingredient	Qty
Bread	6 slices
Eggs	2 nos
Sugar	60 g
Butter	30 g
Milk	250 ml
Nutmeg	a pinch
Cashew nuts	20 g
Sultanas	20 g
Vanilla essence	¼ tsp

Method

1) Butter the bread and cut them into small cubes.
2) Boil milk and cool, add essence and sugar and mix, add nutmeg and essence.
3) Add butter pieces into the milk mixture, add the cashew nuts and sultanas.
4) Grease a mould and put the custard mixture into it.
5) Bake into a pre-heated oven, over hot water after covering with grease proof paper, steam till set.
6) Serve hot.

MENU 4

CONSOMMÉ BRUNOISE

Ingredient	Qty
Brown stock	1 lit

Egg white and shell	1 no
Beef mice	100 g
Onions	50 g
Carrots	30 g
Celery	2 stem chopped
Salt	as reqd
Vinegar	5 ml
Turnips	15 g
Peppercorns	4-5 nos
Bay leaf	2 nos

Method

1) Grate the carrots chop up the onions, celery, and grate the turnips. Cut few brunoise of potatoes and carrots and boil.
2) Add the egg white, mince meat, bay leaf, and peppercorns to the above and mix well stirring constantly, when it is just about to simmer, lower the flame and allow the aft to form.
3) Once the raft is formed, keep the tava under the dechi, and allow to simmer for around ½ an hour.
4) Switch off the flame and strain carefully through a muslin cloth and strain.
5) Serve hot garnished with brunoise of boiled veg.

POMFRET ORLY WITH MAITRE D' HOTE BUTTER

Ingredient	Qty
Pomfret	1 no
Egg	1 no
Flour	60 g
Lime	½ no
Salt and white pepper powder	to taste

Oil	for deep frying the fish
Butter	50 g
Garlic	4-5 nos chopped
Parsley	2 springs chopped finely

Method

1) Clean and cut fish into small fillets, wash well, remove the skin.
2) Make a marinate of lime juice, salt and pepper powder and apply it onto the fish.
3) In a steel bowl mix egg yolk with flour salt and pepper, add water to make a thick paste or batter.
4) Separate the egg white and whip till soft peak form and then fold in the batter.
5) Dip each fish piece in the batter and fry it in hot oil immediately. (golden brown) remove and drain over onto a paper.
6) Serve hot along with maitre d' hote butter.
7) To make the maitre the hote butter mix the butter with finely chopped garlic, lime juice and parsley. Wrap it up in a grease proof paper and keep it in the refrigerator.
8) To serve with the fish, when fish is hot remove a slice of the butter and put onto the hot fish.

PETIT POIS A L FLAMANDE

Ingredient	Qty
Shelled Green Peas	300 g
Carrots	200 g
Butter	50 g
Mint leaves 1 spring	
Salt	to taste
Sugar	a pinch
Pepper powder	to taste

Method

1) Cook the peas in boiling water and drain when tender.
2) Peel wash cut carrots the size of peas and boil them till done strain and keep aside.
3) Melt the butter in a pan toss the carrots, peas together with salt and pepper powder and sugar.
4) Serve hot with the main course as an accompaniment garnished with mint leaves.

CHOCOLATE MOUSSE

Ingredient	*Qty*
Milk	250 ml
Eggs	2 nos
Sugar	60 g
Gelatin	10-15 g
Cocoa powder or	5 g
Melted chocolate	20 g
Cream	50-60 g
Glared cherries	to garnish

Method

1) Mix egg yolk with sugar. Add warm milk and cook over double boiler till you get a custard consistency. (to coat the back of the wooden spoon)
2) Hydrate the gelatine in cold water and then melt it over a hot water and add it into the egg yolk mix.
3) Add cocoa powder and keep stirring over the ice stirring all the time till the mixture turns thick.
4) Fold in stiffly beaten egg white and pour the mixture onto the prepared jelly moulds.
5) To prepare the mould spread lightly oil evenly the inside of the mould this will help to demould the mousse.

6) Refrigerate till set.
7) Decorate it with whipped cream and cream rosette.

MENU 5

CREAM OF SPINACH SOUP

Ingredient	*Qty*
Spinach	1 bunch
Milk	200 ml
Butter	10 g
Flour	10 g
Salt	to taste
Pepper powder	to taste
Water/stock	if required to adjust
Cram	to garnish

Method

1) Make a béchamel sauce of flour, butter and milk.
2) Clean the spinach, wash and immerse them in hot water for approx. 30 secs. Strain.
3) Cool and puree the same. Mix the strained spinach puree into the béchamel sauce and adjust the consistency with water or stock and season the soup with salt and pepper powder.
4) Serve hot garnished with a swirl of cream.

CHICKEN MARENGO

Ingredient	*Qty*
Chicken	1 no
Butter	15 g
Mushrooms	50 g

Bread slices	4 nos
Eggs	4 nos
Garlic	10 g
Shallots	30 g
Stock	250 ml
Tomato concasse	200 ml
Parsley	¼ bunch
Salt	to taste
Pepper powder	to taste
Red flour	50 g
Cray fish	225 g
Oil	to fry

Method

1) Joint the chicken into 4 pieces, season with salt and pepper powder, dredge with flour.
2) Heat butter add chopped garlic and shallots, sauté, add chicken and brown them.
3) Add stock, concassed tomato, sliced mushrooms.
4) Cover the pan and cook till the chicken is tender. (cook in the oven or on the flame)
5) Remove the chicken into a serving dish, pour sauce over it and top with fried egg, surround it with heart shaped fried bread croutons, poached fish.
6) Sprinkle with chopped parsley all around it.

CATEAUX POTATOES

Ingredient	*Qty*
Potatoes	600 g
Butter	25 g
Oil	20 g

Salt	to taste

Method

1) Peel and cut potatoes in even sizes.
2) Par boil them in salted water, drain.
3) Heat butter in a pan along with oil. Toss the potatoes.
4) Finish off in the oven and serve hot as an accompaniment.

CHOCOLATE SOUFFLÉ

Ingredient	*Qty*
Coffee powder	5 g
Milk	60 ml
Sugar	60 g
Eggs	2 nos
Gelatin	10 g
Vanilla essence	¼ tsp
Cream	50 g

Method

1) Warm the milk and dissolve the coffee powder in it.
2) Hydrate the gelatine in water and keep aside.
3) Take 1 full egg and 1 egg yolk and mix it with sugar and whip over a double boiler till thick and fluffy.
4) Whip up the egg ad white till stiff. Whip the cream separately.
5) Melt the hydrated gelatine in hot water, and add it to the egg yolk mixture, add the coffee mixture, vanilla essence, gelatine and mix well.
6) And finally fold the entire mixture into the egg white and half the whipped cream.
7) Pour the mixture into the prepared jelly moulds and refrigerate.

8) When set, demould and decorate it with cream rosette and serve.

MENU 1

MIXED VEGETABLES SOUP

Ingredient	Qty
Potatoes	100 g
Onions	100 g
Carrots	50 g cut into brunoise
Tamato puree	100 g
Salt and white pepper powder	to taste
Stock	1 lit
French beans	20 g cut into lozanes

Method

1) Cut vegetables into their cuts a stock and boil.
2) Sauté onions separately and add into the stock.
3) When vegetables are ¾ done, add in the tomato puree and cook till all the veg. are well done.
4) Season and serve hot.

TOURNADOES BÉARNAISE

Ingredient	*Qty*
Beef undercut	650 g
Oil	50 ml
Salt and white pepper powder	to taste
Brown sauce	2 cups
Vinegar	1 tsp
Red wine	2 tbsp
Mustard paste	½ tsp

Method

1) Clean the beef and cut tournadoes of the undercut (4 nos). remove the trimmings.
2) Make a marinate of salt, pepper powder, vinegar, red wine, mustard paste, and a little oil. Apply the marinate onto the meat and keep it aside for atleast 15-20 mins.
3) Make brown sauce and keep aside.
4) Fry the tournadoes in oil and a little butter on a medium flame to slightly light brown colour, once done put the fried pieces of beef in the brown sauce and continue cooking for another 20 mins.
5) Add the salt and pepper powder if needed.
6) To decorate put a piece of the tournado onto a plate and put some brown sauce, and finally make criss-cross lines of béarnaise sauce onto it.
7) To make the béarnaise sauce make a reduction of white wine (30 ml) crushed peppercorn, and vinegar, strain, add the mixture to the egg yolk (1 nos) add salt and pepper powder to taste. Put this mixture onto a double boiler and gradually add approx. 120 ml of clarified butter. Once done cool and put in a piping bag and use as reqd.

PARSLEY POTATOES

Ingredient	*Qty*
Baby Potatoes	500 g
Butter	25 g
Salt	to taste
White pepper powder	to taste
Parsley	¼ bunch

Method

1) Peel and wash potatoes in their jackets.

2) When done drain, cool and peel.
3) Heat butter in a pan, add salt and add the peeled potatoes. Toss.
4) Mix in the chopped parsley and toss.
5) Serve hot.

MENU 2

CREAM OF MUSHROOM SOUP

Ingredient	Qty
Vegetable stock	1 lit
Mushrooms	100 g
Milk	200 ml
Refined flour	15 g
Butter	15 g
Salt and white pepper powder	to taste
Cream	30 g

Method

1) Clean and wash mushrooms, slice half of them.
2) Puree the remainder of the mushrooms in a little stock and mix the puree up with the remainder of the stock.
3) Make a white sauce and add the puree to it and cook the soup till smooth and thick.
4) Season with salt and pepper and add the sliced mushrooms into it.
5) Add the cream and mix well. Serve hot.

GRILLED CHICKEN

Ingredient	*Qty*
Chicken	1 no
Worshestireshire sauce	2 tsp

Oil	1 tbsp
Mustard paste	½ tsp
Salt and white pepper powder	to taste
Oil	30 ml

Method

1) Joint chicken, clean and wash well.
2) Make a marinade of the above mixture and apply it to the chicken. Keep aside for at least an hour.
3) Heat the griller well and add the chicken to it till the griller effect is seen. Remove and complete the cooking process in the oven.
4) In case of the griller a tava or a frying pan can be used.
5) Remove and serve hot.

CHOCOLATE FUDGE PUDDING

Ingredient	Qty
Ref. flour	150 g
Baking powder	¼ tsp
Sugar	100 g
Margerine/butter	100 g
Cocoa powder	20 g
Milk	50 ml
Sugar	60 g
Milk	50 ml
Cocoa powder	10 g

Method

1) Cream the sugar and marg. Till light and fluffy, when creamed add the sieved flour and cocoa powder and baking powder. Mix in the 50 ml of milk.

2) Mix well. Remove in a baking tray.
3) For the topping mix cocoa powder and sugar and milk sprinkle over the pudding and bake it into a preheated oven for 15-20 mins. At a temp of 180 c, till soft and set.
4) Cool and serve.

MENU 3

MINISTRONI SOUP

Ingredient	Qty
Tomatoes	100 g
Cabbage	50 g
Onions	50 g
Carrots	50 g
Celery	50 g
Parsley	few springs
Macaroni	20 g
Cheese	20 g
Garlic	3-4 flakes
Salt and white pepper powder	as reqd
Oil	15 ml

Method

1) Chop the garlic, cut all the remaining ingredients into tiny equal size pieces, concasse the tomatoes.
2) Fry the garlic in oil. Sauté all the veg. till slightly done, add water and bring to a boil.
3) Add in tomato concasse, and add the macaroni. Cook till done. Adjust the water, season with salt and pepper powder.
4) Garnish with chopped parsley and grated cheese.
5) Serve hot.

POMFRET MUNIERE

Ingredient	*Qty*
Pomfret	1 no (500 g)
Butter	50 g
Oil	20 ml
Flour	50 g
Parsley	few spring
Salt and white pepper powder	to taste
Lime	2 nos

Method

1) Fillet the fish into 4 fillets, wash.
2) Cut one lime into slices and remove the juice of 1 lime. Chop the parsley.
3) Season the fish with salt and pepper powder and dredge in flour.
4) Heat oil and butter in a pan and cook the fish in it.
5) Serve hot. Sprinkle lime juice on top, garnish with lemon slices and parsley. Add remaining butter over the fish.

DIPLOMAT PUDDING

Ingredient	*Qty*
Milk	200 ml
Cream	60 g
Egg yolk	2 nos
Sugar	60 g
Gelatin	20 g
Glucose biscuit	2 nos
Mixed fruit jam	20 g

Vanilla essence	½ tsp
Glazed cherries	5 nos

Method

1) Add the sugar to the egg yolk and mix well.
2) Heat the milk and cool, add it to the egg yolk mix, pit it onto a double boiler and keep stirring till thick. Add the hydrated gelatine to it and mix well.
3) Add vanilla essence and whipped cream, put half the mixture into a prepared jelly mould and put it in a refrigerator and keep for approx 15 mins. Remove and sprinkle with the crushed glucose biscuit, jam and glazed cherries.
4) Pour remaining of the mixture on to the top and refrigerate till set.
5) De mould onto a serving plate and garnish it with glazed cherries.

MENU 4

CABBAGE CHOWDER

Ingredient	*Qty*
Cabbage	250 g
Capsicum	50 g
Flour	30 g
Butter	30 g
Salt and white pepper powder	to taste
Paprika powder	2 g
Cheese	30 g
Water	800 ml
Milk	200 ml
Oil	10 ml

Method

1) Make a bechamel sauce. Keep aside.
2) Wash veg. cut capsicum into ½ inch and deseed, cut juliennes out of capsicum shred cabbage finely.
3) Sauté capsicum and cabbage in oil till light done. Add in the béchamel sauce and water whisk properly.
4) Add grated cheese in the end and simmer till the cheese melts. Serve the chowder hot.

SPAGHETTI NEPOLITAINE

Ingredient	*Qty*
Spaghetti	150 g
Tomato puree	100 ml
Sugar	10 g
Garlic	5-6 nos
Onions	50 g
Salt and white pepper powder	to taste
Oil	20 ml
Paprika powder	2 g

Method

1) Boil water and slat when it is boiling add in the spaghetti and boil till it is just done.
2) Chop garlic and onions, fry till onions become translucent, add in the tomato puree, sugar, salt, pepper powder, and paprika powder cook the sauce.
3) Toss the spaghetti in the nepolitaine sauce and serve hot.

RUSSIAN SALAD

Ingredient	*Qty*
Potatoes	200 g

Carrots	200 g
Green peas	100 g
Mayonnaise sauce	1 cup

Method

1) Make a mayonnaise sauce as given before.
2) Prepare the vegetables, peel wash and cut the potatoes, carrots, into small cubes boil each veg and keep aside.
3) Mix all the veg. in the mayonnaise sauce and keep it in the refrigerator.
4) Serve the salad cold.

FRESH FRUIT SALAD WITH VANILLA CUSTARD

Ingredient	*Qty*
Milk	250 ml
Sugar	60 + 30 g
Vanilla flavoured custard powder	30 g
Banana	2 nos
Apples	50 g
Pineapples	50 g
Cherries	50 g
Strawberries	4 nos cut into quarters

Method

1) Boil the milk with 60 g of sugar, cool remove 20 ml of the milk and add the custard powder and mix well.
2) Once thick, cool, add the cut fruits and mix well.
3) Cool. Serve the fruits salad in an bowl, topped with cherries on top.

MENU 5

CREAM OF TAMATO SOUP

Ingredient	*Qty*
Potatoes	200 g
Onions	100 g
Celery	2 stem
Flour	10 g
Butter	10 g
Milk	100 ml
Parsley	4-5 springs
Salt and pepper powder	to taste

Method

1) Peel and quarter potatoes and onions. Boil in water, with salt. Add a spring of celery.
2) When cooled strain and puree with a little of the pot liquor
3) Strain the puree.
4) Make a béchamel sauce, add the strained puree and heat the soup. Adjust consistency with retained pot liquor.
5) Adjust seasoning with salt and pepper and garnish with very finely chopped celery and parsley.

SCOTCH EGGS

Ingredient	*Qty*
Hard boiled egg	4 nos
Egg	1 no
Mutton or beef mince	250 g
Onions	50 g
Bread crumbs	50 g

Salt and pepper powder	to taste
Oil	to fry
Parsley	few springs
Flour	20 g
Tomato sauce	½ cup

Method

1) Shell hard boiled egg, wash and dry it with the help of a duster and roll over flour and keep aside.
2) Wash mince meat, remove all excess moisture, heat oil add finely chopped onions, mince meat, parsley and adjust the seasonings. Cook well till all the water evaporated and till the meat is cooked.
3) Cool the mixture and then add egg yolk to it and mix well once done, lightly whip the egg white and keep aside.
4) Take the mice meat and place the egg in the centre and shape it into a ball.
5) Roll it in egg white and then over bread crumbs. Continue all the 4 and fry them in hot oil.
6) Serve hot with tomato sauce.
7) For tomato sauce refer the recipe given before.

GREEN SALAD WITH VINAIGRETTE DRESSING

Ingredient	*Qty*
Spring onions	1 no
Lettuce leaves	1 bunch
Tomato	100 g
Red raddish	50 g
Cucumber	100 g
Carrots	100 g
Black olives	4 nos

Green olives	4 nos
Salt	as reqd
White pepper powder	as reqd
Oil	10 ml
Vinegar	10 ml

Method

1) Cut up the vegetables decoratively. Wash veg. Well before cutting.
2) Arrange the veg. decoratively on to a platter/plate.
3) Make a dressing out of salt, pepper powder, oil and vinegar. Mix well.
4) Pour over the salad just before serving.
5) Serve the salad cold.

BANANA FRITTERS

Ingredient	*Qty*
Bananas	2 nos
Powdered sugar	100 g
Egg	1 no
Flour	60 g
Oil	to deep fry
Soda bi carb	a pinch

Method

1) Cut the bananas into 6 pieces.
2) Make a fritter batter with the egg yolk and refined flour, soda and water. Mix till thick, incorporate stiffly beaten egg white with 15 g powdered sugar into the batter.
3) Heat oil, dip bananas into the batter and fry well till golden brown. Remove into a grease proof paper and sprinkle with powdered sugar while still hot over the fritters.
4) Serve warm.

TOMATO SHORBA

Ingredient	*Qty*
Tomato	250 g
Pepper corns	4-5 nos
Bay leaf	2 nos
Cinnamon	1 g
Kasturi methi	2 g
Ginger and garlic	10 + 10 g
Mint	3-4 springs
Corriander leaves	1/4th bunch
Sugar	as reqd
Lime	1 no
Carrots	20 g
Onions	50 g

Method

1) Wash tomatoes, cut into large pieces, grate carrots, chop tomatoes.
2) Place all ingredients in a heavy bottomed pan. Add spring of mint, bring to a boil and then simmer for around an hour.
3) When the shorba attains body, take it off the fire and strain through a muslin cloth.
4) Adjust seasoning, add lime juice and garnish with chopped coriander leaves and mint leaves.
5) Serve piping hot.

SHAHI PANEER

Ingredient	*Qty*
Paneer	250 g
Curd	259 g

Ginger garlic paste	20 g
Poppy seed paste	20 g
Onions	100 g
Cashew nuts	50 g
Green chilli paste	10 g
Garam masala powder	2 g
Full garam masala powder	2 g
Oil	50 ml
Salt	to taste

Method

1) Cut paneer into equal sized cubes and keep it in salted water.
2) Cut and boil onions, strain and puree.
3) Boil, poppy seeds and cashew nuts in water and when softened, puree grind them.
4) Fry the garam masala and add the green chilli paste to it, add ginger garlic paste.
5) Add the poppy seed pate and cook for sometime. Add cashew nut paste, onion paste, and beaten curds.
6) Heat and keep whisking, if there is a need add little water. Finally add in the paneer pieces and cook for a while and sprinkle garam masala powder. Mix well.
7) Serve hot.

ROTI

Ingredient	*Qty*
Whole wheat flour (Atta)	250 g
Salt	as reqd
Water	as reqd
Fat/oil	50 g

Method

1) Make a soft dough using the above ingredients, except fat, and rest the dough the dough for at least an hour.
2) Divide the dough into individual portion and roll it out into a round disc.
3) Roast it onto a tawa on both sides and smear it with fat.
4) Serve hot with subji or curry.

BOONDI RAITA

Ingredient	*Qty*
Khara boondi	100 g
Curd	250 g
Sugar	to taste
Salt	to taste
Red chilli powder	5 g
Corriander leaves	to garnish

Method

1) Chop corriander leaves, soak *boondi* in warm water.
2) Whip the curd, add chili powder, sugar and salt.
3) Remove water from the *boondi* by squeezing them, add the boondi to the whipped curd.
4) Garnish with chopped coriander leaves and chilli powder.
5) Serve chilled.

PARSI MENU 2

BROWN RICE

Ingredients	*Qty*
Rice	500 gms
Sugar	5 gm

Cloves	2 gm
Cardamom	2 gm
Peppercorns	2 gm
Salt	TT
Oil	50 ml
Onions	50 gm

Method

1. Pick rice. Chop onions and fry till dark brown.
2. Add whole garam masala to the browned onions till they splutter.
3. Add sugar and caramelize till dark brown.
4. Add 1½ times water.
5. Add washed rice to the boiling mixture.
6. Put the degchi over a tawa and lower the flame. Cover the let the rice cook.
7. Add more water only if required.
8. Rice is done when soft (but not mashy). Remove from fire and serve hot with dhansak dal

DHANSAK DAL

Ingredients	*Qty*
Toor dal	250 gm
Dhansak masala	20 gm
Onions	150 gms
Green chillies2-3 nos	
Tomatoes	50 gm
Pumpkin	25 gm
Brinjals	25 gm
Curry leaves	1 spring
Coriander leaves	1 bunch
Chilli powder	5 gm

Dhania powder	10 gm
Jeera powder	10 gm
Haldi powder	2 gm
Salt	TT
Oil	100 ml
Mutton/chicken	500 gms
Ginger garlic paste	15 gm

Method:

1. Pick and soak dal for 4-5 hours.
2. Clean and cut meat/chicken and wash. Apply salt and keep.
3. Chop onions and fry till light brown. Add chilli and curry leaves. Add ginger garlic paste, chilli paste, haldi, dhania, jeera powder, dhansak masala and sauté all masalas in a cooker.
4. Add chopped tomatoes and cook with the masalas add chopped fresh coriander.
5. Add mutton/chicken and seas on a high flame. Add washed dal, salt and water.
6. Close the cooker and let the dal and meat cook well for 3-4 whistles on a medium flame.
7. When cooked remove out the meats and whistle the dal till smooth. Adjust the consistency with hot water if required.
8. Serve the meat and dal hot with brown rice as the accompaniments and onions and tomatoes cucumber.

SALI MURG*

Ingredients	*Qty*
Boneless mutton	500 gms
Onions	250 gms

*Name of the dish is 'Sali Mung' but mutton is used.

Tomatoes	300 gms
Coriander leaves	½ bunch
Ginger garlic paste	15 gm
Red chilli paste	5 gm
Dates	150 gms
Green chillies	2-3 nos
Haldi powder	a pinch
Dhania powder	10 gm
Jeera powder	10 gm
Salt	TT
Oil	75 ml
Sali	100 gm

Method

1. Clean and cut the mutton into ¾" cubes wash and apply salt and ginger garlic and red chilli paste.
2. Chop onions and fry till brown. Cool and make a paste.
3. Remove puree of the tomatoes and strain the liquid to get rid of the seeds.
4. Deseed dates and make a thick paste.
5. Heat oil add chopped green chilies, ginger, garlic, red chilli paste and dry masalas. Add onion paste, date paste and tomato puree and chopped coriander leaves, salt and marinated mutton. Seal the met, add water and cook.
6. When mutton is cooked, adjust consistency of gravy and salt. The gravy should be fairly thick.
7. Serve meat with gravy and sprinkles Sali (potatoes allumets) on top and serve with thin chapattis.

PUMPKIN SALAD

Ingredients	*Qty*
Red pumpkin	¼ kg (1½ lbs)

Finely chopped onion	1½ tbsp
Finely chopped coriander	1½ tbsp
Finely chopped chilli	1½ tbsp
Plain yoghurt	4-6 tbsp
Salt	TT

Method

1. Remove seed section from pumpkin. Remove skin. Cut pumpkin into small pieces and put in a pan with ¼ cup water and the salt and cook, covered, till pumpkin is very soft. Uncover pan and continue cooking till pumpkin is as dry as possible.
2. Mash pumpkin to a smooth pulp with a potato masher or fork, then put into a serving dish. Refrigerate.
3. Just before serving add the remaining ingredients and mix well.

GUJRATI MENU 3

PEELA BHAT

Ingredients	*Qty*
Basmati rice	1½ cups
Ghee	1½ tbsp
Cloves	5
Cinnamon	1½
Turmeric powder	¾ tsp
Water	2½ cups
Salt	TT

Preparation

The rice: Rinse thoroughly at least twice and soak for 45 min. Drain off the water and set aside.

Method

1. Bring the 2½ cups of water to a boil. In the meanwhile heat the ghee and add cloves and cinnamon. Once they crackle, add the rice. Sauté the rice and once it starts sticking to be bottom of the pan. Add the boiling water, turmeric and salt.
2. Place the vessel of rice in the cooker and pressure cook on a high flame for two whistles. Turn of the stove immediately. Remove the rice once the pressure subsides.

To reserve:

Remove the rice onto a platter or serving plate and serve hot.

GUJRATHI DAL

Ingredients	*Qty*
Split red gram	100 gm
Green chillies	6 gm
Ginger	5 gm
Turmeric	1 gm
Jaggery	13-15 gm
Salt	TT
Cocum	3-4
Tamarind	15 gm
Water	1 lit
Oil	15 ml
To temper:	
Mustard	1 gm
Fenugreek	1 gm
Asafetida	1 gm

Method

1. Boil the gram in water till well cooked.
2. Mash well.
3. Add sliced green chillies, ginger, turmeric, salt, tamarind juice or cocum and jaggery.
4. Boil for half an hour over slow fire. Remove.
5. Heat oil in a frying pan.
6. Add mustard seeds, fenugreek and asafetida.
7. As the seeds splutter, pour over dal.
8. Mix well.

NB: Split black gram (urad dal) can be substituted for red gram. Use 30 gm of curds beater up in a cup of water instead of tamarind or cocum and reduce jaggery to 10 gm.

LASUN KI CHUTNEY

Ingredeitns	*Qty*
Dry coconut	75 gm
Red chilli	100 gm
Garlic	75 gm
Dill seed	75 gm
Roasted groundnut	30 gm
Cumin powder	5 gm
Salt	to taste

Method

1. Deseed whole red chillies.
2. Clean garlic
3. Combine all the ingredients and grind coarsely.
4. Check for seasoning with salt.

OONDHIU

The epitome of gujrathi cuisine. Oondhiu is a vegetable medley with fenugreek leaf dumplings. It is usually prepared in winter when fresh vegetable like surti papad are in abundance.

Preparation time	1 hour 30 min
Cooking time	1 hour
Ingredients	*Qty*
Yam	100 gm
Potatoes (lemon sized)	350 gms
Brinjals	200 gms
Banns	3 ripe
Surti papad	250 gms
Oil	8-10 tbsp
Salt	TT
For the filling:	
Coconut	115 gm
Coriander leaves	½ cup
Garlic	2-3
Ginger	½ pieces
Green chillies	5
Sugar	2 tbsp
Asafetida	¼ tsp
Soda bicarbonate	¼ tsp
Salt	TT
For the dumplings:	
Fenugreek leaves	1 bunch
Turmeric powder	½ tsp

Chilli powder	2 tsp
Lime	1
Bengal gram flour	115 gms
Oil	2 tbsp hot

Preparation

The **yam and sweet potatoes**: Peel and cut into 1" cubes.

The **potatoes**: Peel and cut their length.

The **brinjals**: Remove stems and slit into quarters to halfway down their length.

The **bananas**: Cut into two pieces without removing the skin, slit each of the two piece into quarters halfway down their length.

The **fenugreek leaves**: Clean sprinkle with 1 teaspoon salt and set aside. The salt helps to remove the bitterness form the fenugreek leaves.

The **coconut**: grate and set aside.

The **beans**: Thread wash and set aside.

The **coriander leaves**: Chop, wash and set aside.

The **garlic**: Remove the skin and finely chop. Set aside.

The **dumplings**; Mix the fenugreek leaves, a pinch of turmeric powder, chilli powder, gram flour, hot oil and salt to taste.

Add water little by little to form a stiff paste. Make balls of this paste and deep fry in hot oil till golden brown and set aside.

The **filling**: Mix the grated coconut, chopped coriander leaves, garlic, ground ginger, green chillies, sugar, soda bicarbonate, asafetida and salt together.

Method

1. Divide the above mixture into three portions. Stuff the

brinjals, potatoes, bananas with 2 potions. Smear the yam and the sweet potatoes with the remaining third setting aside 2 teaspoons of the filling mixture. Sauté well.

2. Add 2 cups of water and bring to a boil. Then add the beans and a pinch of soda bicarbonate. Cover the pan with a lid and cook over a low flame for 5-6 min. add the stuffed brinjals and cook with lid on for another 10-15 min. add the potatoes, sweet potatoes and yam cubes, cook with lid on over a low flame until all the vegetables are done. When nearly done add fried gram balls and stuffed bananas. Cover and simmer for 3 min. when the preparation is done, the fat will separated.

To serve

Serve hot with rotis

BOHRI MENU 4

DAL GOSHT

Ingredients	*Qty*
Mutton	½ kg
Tur dal	½ cup
Masoor dal	½ cup
Gram dal	½ cup
Turmeric powder	½ tsp
Hara masala	2 tbsp
Finely chopped onions	2
Red chilli powder	2 tsp
Coriander powder	2 tsp
Cumin powder	2 tsp
Garam masala powder	¼ tsp
Fenugreek leaves	1 tbsp
Coriander leaves	½ cup

Cloves 4
Peppercorns 8
Cinnamon 2" piece
T tbsp cumin
Curry leaves few
Clime 1
Salt TT

Method

1. In a cooker put mutton, dals, onion, tomatoes, hara masalas, turmeric and salt. 1 tbsp oil and add 2 cups of water and pressure cook. In another pan, heat oil and add whole garam masala, add curry leaves and cumin. When it crackles, add the dal and then all the dry masalas. When boiled, add lime juice and garnish with fenugreek leaves and coriander leaves chopped. Serve hot with jeera rice or tandoori roti.

KANDA BATATA

Ingredients	Qty
Sliced onions	¼ kg
Medium sized tomatoes	2
Potatoes sliced	¼ kg
Hara masala	2 tsp
Red chilli powder	2 tsp
Coriander cumin powder	4 tsp
Oil	½ cup
Salt	TT

Method:

Heat the oil and then add onion and potatoes, tomatoes, dry masalas, hara masalas and salt. Do not stir. Cover the vessel and cook on a slow flame for 2-4 min. open and stir. Cook again for another 10 min. serve with roti or moong ki khichdi.

MINT CHUTNEY

Ingredients	Qty
Chopped mint leaves	1 cup
Coriander leaves	½ cup
Curd	200 ml
Green chillies	2-3
Salt, cumin and sugar	½

Method

Grind all the ingredients into a fine paste. Whip curd add the chutney to it. Serve with sheek kabab.

SHEER KURMA

Ingredients	Qty
Mava	100 gm
Ghee	2 tbsp
Sev (vermicelli)	100 gms
Water	1 cup
Cardamom powder	¼ tsp
Ground almonds & pistachios	2 tbsp
Sugar	1 cup
Charoli 30 gms	
Raisins	30 gms

Method

Boil milk and reduce to 1 litre. Clean raisins and set aside. Heat ghee, fry serve till it is golden brown. Then add raisins and fry for 1 min. add 1 cup water. Bring to a boil, add hot milk and cook till it thickens. Add sugar and mava and boil for another 5 min. Finally add almond-pistachio powder and charoli. Serve hot.

9

Oven and Broiler Meals

OVEN MEALS

COMPANY CHICKEN

1 packaged frozen chicken breasts and thighs, thawed

Flour, salt, pepper.

Shortening

1 can cream of chicken soup

½ teaspoon curry powder

1-4 ounce can sliced mushrooms

Flour and season chicken. In skillet, brown thoroughly on all sides in shortening on medium high heat. Place chicken in large casserole. Add soup to pan in which chicken was fried; stir to pick up drippings. Add curry and mushrooms. Pour over chicken, cover, and bake.

Temp: 350°F

Time: 50 Minutes

Serves: 6

OVEN-FRIED POTATOES

Pare 6 potatoes; slice ¼ inch thick; toss in ½ cup melted butter to coat thoroughly. Put in baking dish; salt and pepper; pour remaining butter over potatoes. Bake.

Temp: 350°F

Time: 50 Minutes

Serves: 6

BUTTERED CARROTS

Peel and slice carrots into casserole.

Salt and pepper, top with butter, add ¼ cup water. Cover and bake.

Temp: 350°F

Time: 50 Minutes

Serves: 6

CHOCOLATE-BROWNIE PIE

2 squared unsweetened chocolate

2 tablespoons butter

3 eggs

½ cup sugar

¾ cup dark corn syrup

¾ cup pecans

1 9" unbaked pie shell

Melt chocolate and butter. Add eggs, sugar and corn syrup, beating thoroughly. Mix in pecans. Pour filling into unbaked pie shell. Bake with oven meal.

Temp: 350°F

Time: 50 Minutes

Serves: 6

BRAISED SPICY STEAK

2 lbs. round steak ½ inch thick

¼ cup flour

1 teaspoon salt

¼ teaspoon pepper

3 tablespoons shortening

1 cup catsup

½ cup water

1 onion and 1 lemon

1 green pepper, cut into rings

5 whole cloves

Dredge steak with flour mixed with seasonings; pound in slightly. Melt shortening in frypan; brown meat on both sides on medium high heat. Put in baking pan. Mix catsup and water; pour over meat. Top with thinly sliced onion and lemon; green pepper, and cloves. Cover with foil and bake.

Temp: 350°F

Time: 50 Minutes

Serves: 6

STEAMED RICE IN CONSOMMÉ

Brown 1 cup uncooked rice in 3 tablespoons butter in skillet on medium heat. Out in 1½ quart casserole. Combine 1 can consommé, 1 can water and ½ teaspoon salt; add to rice. Cover and bake.

Temp: 350°F

Time: 50 Minutes

Serves: 6

GREEN BEANS AND SCALLIONS

Cut stems off 1 bunch scallions, and finely chop 2 inches of stems. Cook in covered casserole with 2 packages frozen green beans, salt, butter and ½ cup water. Stir about halfway through.

Temp: 350°F

Time: 50 Minutes

Serves: 6

DATE TOPPED CAKE

Cake ingredients:

1 cup chopped cake

1 teaspoon soda

1 cup boiling water

$1^1/_3$ cups sifted flour

1 teaspoon baking powder

1/8 teaspoon salt

1 cup sugar

1 egg beater

1 tablespoon melted butter

½ cup chopped nuts

Date topping ingredients:

½ cup chopped nut meats

1 cup sugar

$^2/_3$ cup boiling water

1 cup chopped dates

Pit and cut up dates; add soda dissolved in boiling water, and let stand. Sift flour with baking powder, salt and sugar; add-to chopped dates along with beater egg and butter. Mix well; stir in chopped nuts. Bake in 8 inch greased pan.

Temp: 350°F

Time: 50 Minutes

Serves: 6

Date topping:

Combine ½ cup chopped nut meats, 1 cup sugar, 2/3 boiling water, and 1 cup chopped dates. Pour over cake as soon as it comes from oven. Let cake cool in pan.

BAKED HAM SLICES WITH WALNUT STUFFING

4 cups bread crumbs

2 tablespoons melted shortening

1 egg

1 teaspoon poultry seasoning

1/8 teaspoon pepper

1 cup chopped celery

¼ cup chopped onions

¾ cup broken walnuts

1 1-inch slices tenderized ham

Combine stuffing ingredients. Score ham. Place one slice in baking dish; cover with stuffing. Put second slice of ham on top. Secure with toothpicks; bake.

Temp: 350°F

Time: 1 Hour

Serves: 6

BUTTERED BROCCOLI

Place 2 packages frozen broccoli spears in 2 quart casserole; add ¼ cup water. Salt, dot with butter. Cover and bake. Turn pieces of broccoli about halfway through cooking period.

Temp: 350°F

Time: 1 Hour

Serves: 6

Pineapple-apple crunch

5 medium apples

1 small can crushed pineapple

1 cup brown sugar

3 tablespoons cornstarch

½ teaspoon salt

¼ teaspoon cinnamon

2 tablespoon butter

Peal, core and slice apples; place in buttered baking dish in layers with pineapple. Mix dry ingredients and sprinkle over top. Dot with butter and bake.

Temp: 350°F

Time: 1 Hour

Serves: 6

HAM LOAF

1 pound veal, ground

1 pound smoked ham, ground

4 tablespoons catsup

3 tablespoons chopped green pepper

1 small onion, chopped

1 cup mushrooms, stems and pieces

2 eggs, beater

½ cup milk

1/8 teaspoon pepper

1 cup cracker crumbs

Mix ingredients; pack into greased loaf pan. Bake.

Temp: 375°F

Time: 1 Hour

Serves: 6

ITALIAN GREEN BEANS WITH ONIONS

Place 2 packages frozen Italian green beans and ¼ cup water in 1½ quart casserole. Add 1 small onion, grated; salt, pepper, and butter. Cover and bake. Stir about halfway through cooking period.

Temp: 375°F

Time: 1 Hour

Serves: 6

EASY NUT BREAD

½ cup sugar

1 egg

1½ cups milk

1½ cups chopped nuts

3 cups biscuit mix

Blend first four ingredients. Stir in biscuit mix. Beat 30 seconds. Pour into greased 1-pound loaf pan. Bake.

Temp: 375°F

Time: 1 Hour

Serves: 6

APPLE CRISP

4 to 6 cups sliced apples

1 cup sugar

½ cup rolled oats

½ cup flour

1 teaspoon cinnamon

½ cup melted butter

Place apples in greased glass baking dish. Combine dry ingredients and work in melted butter. Sprinkle over apples and bake.

Temp: 375°F

Time: 1 Hour

Serves: 6

BAKED SALMON

800 gram pieces fresh salmon

1 cup sour cream

1 teaspoon salt

Pepper

2 tablespoons grated onion

2 tablespoons chopped parsley

Put fish in greased baking pan. Mix all but parsley; pour over salmon and bake. Serve sprinkled with parsley.

Temp: 375°F

Time: 1 Hour

Serves: 4

POTATOES AU GRATIN

2 cups white sauce (Bechamel sauce)

2½ cups grated American cheese

1 teaspoon grated onion

3 cups cooked diced potatoes

Salt and pepper

Make medium white sauce. Stir in 1½ cups grated cheese and onion. Place 1 cup potatoes in greased casserole. Sprinkle with salt and pepper. Pour on about 1/3 of the cheese sauce. Repeat layer twice. Sprinkle remaining grated cheese on top. Cover and bake.

Temp: 375°F

Time: 1 Hour

Serves: 4

ITALIAN ZUCCHINI

8 medium Zucchini squash

1 No. 2 can whole tomatoes

1 tablespoon chopped green pepper

I medium onion, sliced

Salt and pepper

Butter

Cut Zucchini in half lengthwise; place in casserole. Pour tomatoes over squash. Sprinkle on green pepper and place onion slices on top. Season with salt and pepper; dot with butter. Cover and bake.

Temp: 375°F

Time: 1 Hour

Serves: 4

STUFFED BAKED APPLES

4 baking apples

½ cup raisings

½ cup brown sugar

½ teaspoon cinnamon

¼ teaspoon salt

¼ cup chopped nuts

Core apples, place in baking pan. Mix raisins, brown sugar, cinnamon, salt and chopped nuts together. Fill apples with mixture. Pour 1 cup water around apples and bake.

Temp: 375°F

Time: 1 Hour

Serves: 4

BARBECUED BEEF PATTIES

1 cup soft bread crumbs

c cup milk

1 pound ground beef

1 teaspoon salt

Pepper

1½ tablespoon Worcestershire sauce

¼ cup vinegar

3 tablespoon sugar

½ cup catsup

½ cup water

½ cup chopped onion

½ cup chopped green pepper

Moisten crumbs with milk; combine with beef, salt, pepper, and other ingredients. Shape into 4 patties. Put in baking dish. Combine remaining ingredients; pour over patties, bake.

Temp: 350°F

Time: 50 Minutes

Serves: 4

POTATOES IN SOUR CREAM

4 cooked potatoes, diced finely diced

1 small onion, diced

1½ teaspoon salt

¼ teaspoon pepper

1 cup sour cream

Combine potatoes with onion. Place 1/3 mixture in

greased 1½ quart casserole. Season with salt, pepper; dot with sour cream. Repeat layers twice; end with sour cream. Bake.

Temp: 350°F

Time: 50 Minutes

Serves: 4

BRUSSELS SPROUTS

In casserole, place 1 package frozen sprouts, ¼ cup water, ¼ cup parmesan cheese, butter, salt and pepper, cover; bake.

Temp: 350°F

Time: 50 Minutes

Serves: 4

CRUSTY GINGERBREAD

½ cup shortening

½ cup sugar

1 egg

¾ cup molasses

2 cups sifted flour

2 teaspoons baking powder

¼ teaspoon soda

½ teaspoon salt

1 teaspoon ginger

¾ cup buttermilk

1 tablespoon melted butter

3 tablespoons grated orange rind

½ cup chopped nuts

Cream shortening, sugar. Add egg, beat well; stir in molasses. Sift together dry ingredients; add alternately with buttermilk to creamed mixture beginning and ending with dry ingredients. Pour into greased 8-inch square pan. Combine butter, sugar, rind, and nuts, sprinkle over batter, and bake.

Temp: 350°F

Time: 50 Minutes

Serves: 4

BEEF IN SOUR CREAM

2 pounds round steak

¼ cup shortening

1 large onion, diced

1 clove garlic, minced

1 can (4 oz.) sliced mushrooms, undrained

1 (8 oz.) can tomato sauce

¾ cup beef bouillon

1 tablespoon Worcestershire sauce

1 teaspoon salt

1/8 teaspoon pepper

1½ cups dairy sour cream

Cut steak in 1-inch cubes. Heat shortening on surface unit medium high setting. Add onion and garlic and sauté until onions yellow; add meat and brown well on all sides. Pour off any fat; add remaining ingredients and blend. Cover and bake in 2 quart casserole in oven for 11/4 hours.

Temp: 325°F

Time: 11/4 Hours

Serves: 4-6

Tip: This is a very good dish when you're entertaining because it is ready to serve when it comes form the oven. No slicing or last minute touches are needed.

BAKED NOODLES

8 ounces noodles, uncooked (about 5 cups)

1 teaspoon salt

¼ cup butter

4 cups boiling water

Spread noodles in 2-quart casserole, add remaining ingredients, and stir well. Cover and bake.

Temp: 325°F

Time: 11/4 Hours

Serves: 4-6

Tip: This is especially good with a main dish such as Beef in Sour cream because the noodles are relatively bland to go with a flavourful main dish.

PEACH-BLUEBERRY CRUMBLE

1 can (1 lb.) sliced peaches

1 pkg. (13½ oz.) blueberry muffin mix

½ cup flour

½ cup sugar

½ teaspoon nutmeg

¼ cup butter

1 tablespoon lemon juice

Drain peaches and blueberries (from muffin mix) reserving 2 tablespoons blueberry liquid. Prepare mix according to package directions, and spread in greased 2 quart (11½ X 7½ X 1½ inch) baking dish. Arrange peaches on batter in even rows. Combine blueberries, reserved blueberry liquid, and lemon juice and spread over peaches. Combine flour, sugar and nutmeg; cut in butter until mixture is crumbly. Sprinkle crumb mixture over fruit. Bake.

Temp: 325°F

Time: 11/4 Hours

Serves: 4-6

Tip: This can be prepared quickly from ingredients you can keep on hand – a real help when unexpected guests arrive.

BAKED HAM SLICE

Ham slice, 1½ inches thick

Whole cloves

¼ cup orange juice

2 tablespoons lemon juice

½ cup honey

2 tablespoons prepared mustard

1 tablespoon cornstarch

1 tablespoon water

¼ cup raisins

1 orange, peeled and cut into bite size pieces

Score fat edge of ham and stud with cloves; place in 2½ quart (13½ x 8½ x 1½ inch) baking dish. Combine citrus juices, honey and mustard and pour over ham. Cover and bake, when ready to serve, transfer ham to serving platter and keep warm. Pour juice from baking dish into saucepan. Combine cornstarch and water and stir into juice from ham. Cook on medium heat until sauce thickens, boils and is clear and glossy. Add raising and cook 2 to 3 minutes longer; add orange pieces and serve hot over ham slice.

Temp: 350° F

Time: 1 Hour

Serves: 4

SWEET POTATO FANS

4 medium sweet potatoes

2 tablespoons water

2 tablespoons butter

Nutmeg

Pare sweet potatoes and cut cross-wise into ¼ inch thick slices. Place in 1 quart baking dish, drizzle with water, and dot with butter. Sprinkle with nutmeg. Cover and bake.

Temp: 350°F

Time: 1 Hour

Serves: 4

Tip: Sweet potatoes are a natural compliment to ham.

CORN-CELERY CASSEROLE

2 pkgs. (10 oz. each) frozen corn

1 can celery soup, undiluted

½ teaspoon salt

¼ cup chopped pimiento/Pimento

Combine corn (thaw slightly, if necessary) soup, salt, and pimiento in 2 quart casserole. Cover and bake.

Temp: 350°F

Time: 1 Hour

Serves: 4

Tip: celery soup makes a quick and easy sauce for this creamed corn with a new twist.

CRAB GIOVANNI

About 4 oz. spaghetti

¼ cup butter

1 cup chopped onion

1 can (4 oz.) sliced mushrooms, drained

1 clove garlic, minced

1 can (9 oz.) crab meat

¼ cup sliced stuffed green olives

¼ cup shredded cheddar cheese

¼ cup diary sour cream

1 can (1 lb.) tomatoes

½ teaspoon salt

¼ teaspoon basil

Cook spaghetti according to package directions. Melt butter in skillet on medium setting. When butter is hot, add onion, mushrooms, and garlic and saute until onion yellows. Combine with remaining ingredients and mix well. Pour into a 2 quart casserole, cover and bake.

Temp: 325°F

Time: 1 Hour

Serves: 6-8

BUTTERED BROCCOLI

2 pkgs. Frozen broccoli

½ cup water

½ teaspoon salt

Place ingredients in 1½ quart casserole. Cover and bake.

Temp: 325°F

Time: 1 Hour

Serves: 6-8

Cherry pudding cake

2 tablespoons butter

½ cup sugar

1 egg

1 cup flour

1½ teaspoons baking powder

½ teaspoon salt

½ cup milk

1 can (1 lb.) sour red cherries

½ cup sugar

1/8 teaspoon almond extract

Red food colouring (optional)

Blend butter and ½ cup sugar; add egg and blend. Combine flour, baking powder and salt, add alternately with milk to creamed mixture and mix just until batter smooth. Spread batter in greased 2 quart (11½ × 7½ × 1½ inch) baking dish. Drain cherries, reserving liquid. Add enough water to the cherry liquid to make 1½ cups, combine with remaining ½ cup sugar in saucepan and bring to a boil. Remove from heat and add almond extract and food colouring if desired. Arrange cherries over cake batter, and pour hot syrup over cherries. Place in oven and bake for one hour or until cake springs back when pressed lightly with finger. Serve hot or cold with ice cream or whipped cream.

Temp: 325°F

Time: 1 Hour

Serves: 6-8

Tip: Frozen cherries can be substituted, but if sweetened cherries are used, omit the second ½ cup of sugar.

VEAL SCALLOPINI

2 pounds boned veal shoulder

½ cup flour

½ teaspoon salt

¼ teaspoon pepper

½ cup cooking oil

½ cup minced onion

1 8 oz. can whole mushrooms, drained

1 No. 303 can (2 cups) tomatoes

1 teaspoon sugar

1½ teaspoons salt

¼ teaspoon pepper

Cut veal into 11/4" cubes; roll lightly in flour combined with ½ teaspoon salt, ¼ teaspoon pepper. In hot cooking oil in skillet, sauté (on top unit control at 300°F) onions until tender but not brown. Remove onions to greased 2 quart casserole. Sauté veal in oil left in skillet until brown on all sides, place in 2 quart casserole along with mushrooms and tomatoes. Sprinkle sugar, salt and pepper over the top. Bake covered in a preheated 350°F oven for one hour and 15 minutes.

Serve with rice.

Temp: 350°F

Time: 1 Hour 15 minutes

Serves: 4-6

OVEN RICE

1¼ cups converted, long grain rice

1 teaspoon salt

2½ cups boiling water

2¼ tablespoons butter

Grease a 1½ quart casserole. Add rice, salt, boiling water and butter. Cover tightly with foil. Bake in preheated 350°F oven for one hour and 15 minutes.

Temp: 350°F

Time: 1 Hour 15 minutes

Serves: 4-6

PECAN PIE

½ cup sugar

¼ cup butter

1 cup light corn syrup

¼ teaspoon salt

3 eggs

1 cup pecan meats

1 recipe plain pastry

Cream sugar and butter together until fluffy and light. Add syrup and salt; beat well. Add eggs, one at a time and beat one minute after each addition. Stir in pecans. Pour into unbaked pie shell and bake in a preheated 350°F oven for one hour and 15 minutes.

Temp: 350°F

Time: 1 Hour 15 minutes

Serves: 4-6

PIE CRUST

11/4 cups sifted all purpose flour

¾ teaspoon salt

½ cup shortening

3 tablespoons cold water

Mix together the flour and slat. Cut in shortening until size of crumbs resembles small peas. Sprinkle water over mixture. Gently mix with a fork until the particles cling together to form a dough. Shape into a ball on a floured (1 tablespoon) wax paper sheet. Roll with light strokes in a circle one inch wider than the pie pan. Fit into a 9" pie pan. Yield 6 servings.

HAMBURGER PIE

5 medium potatoes, cooked

Milk

1 beaten egg

1 pound ground beef

1 medium onion, chopped

¾ teaspoon salt

Dash pepper

1 1-pound can (2 cups) cut green beans drained, or ½ pound green beans, cooked and drained or 1 9-ounce package frozen green beans, cooked and drained

1 10½-ounce can condensed tomato soup undiluted

1 8-ounce can of tomato sauce

Mash potatoes while hot with milk, blend in egg; set aside. Lightly brown meat, onion and seasonings (on top unit control at 325°F). Add drained beans, soup and tomato sauce; pour into a greased 2 quart casserole. Drop mashed potato topping in mounds over meat mixture. Bake uncovered in preheated 400°F oven for 45 minutes.

Temp: 400°F

Time: 45 Minutes

Serves: 4-6

BAKED APPLES

6 medium size baking apples

6 tablespoons brown sugar

2 tablespoon butter

Wash apples; remove core. Place in baking dish. Put in the center of each apple one tablespoon brown sugar and ½ teaspoon butter. Pour 1 cup water around apples and bake uncovered in preheated 400°F oven for 45 minutes.

Temp: 400°F

Time: 45 Minutes

Serves: 4-6

OVEN BARBECUED CHICKEN

1 3-lb. fryer, disjointed

1 cup water

½ cup catsup

3 tablespoons brown sugar

1 tablespoon Worcestershire sauce

1½ teaspoon salt

1/8 teaspoon chilli powder

Arrange chicken in a single layer skin side up in a roasting pan. Combine all ingredients and pour over chicken. Bake uncovered in a preheated 400°F oven for one hour. Yield: 4-6 servings.

Temp: 400°F

Time: 1 Hour

Serves: 4-6

PAN ROASTED POTATOES

6 medium size potatoes

½ cup butter, melted

Pare potatoes and precook 10 minutes in boiling salted water to cover. Drain and arrange potatoes in a single layer in 1½ quart baking dish. Pour butter over potatoes. Roll each piece to coat with the butter. Bake uncovered in preheated 400°F oven for one hour. Yield: 6 servings.

Temp: 400°F

Time: 1 Hour

Serves: 4-6

ONIONS EN CASSEROLE

6 medium onions

1/3 cup strained honey

¼ cup water

3 tablespoons butter (½ T. per onion)

Peel and wash onions and arrange in single layer in 1 quart baking dish. Mix together honey and water; pour over onions, dot with butter. Cover and bake in preheated 400°F oven for one hour.

Temp: 400°F

Time: 1 Hour

Serves: 4-6

SALMON LOAF

1 1-pound can salmon (2 cups) drained

1 cup dry bread crumbs

½ cup finely chopped celery

1 egg, slightly beaten

¾ teaspoon salt

1 tablespoon lemon juice

2 tablespoons butter

2 tablespoons flour

1½ cups milk

Add the bread crumbs, celery, egg, salt and lemon juice to the salmon. Mix lightly. In a saucepan melt butter (on top unit control at 200°F). Blend flour into butter; add milk gradually, stirring constantly. Cook until thickened and smooth. Blend this white sauce into the salmon mixture. Bake in a greased 9 × 5 x 23/4" loaf pan in preheated 325°F oven for one hour.

Temp: 325°F

Time: 1 Hour

Serves: 6-8

FLUFFY POTATO CASSEROLE

4 or 5 medium potatoes

Hot milk

1/3 cup shredded process sharp cheese

½ cup heavy cream, whipped

Pare potatoes and cook in boiling water for 30 minutes, drain and mash. Season mashed potatoes with salt and pepper; add sufficient hot milk to ship lightly. Pile into greased 1½ quart (round) casserole. Fold shredded cheese into whipped cream and spread over potatoes. Bake in a preheated 325°F oven for oven for one hour.

Temp: 325°F

Time: 1 Hour

Serves: 6-8

FRUIT COMPOTE

2½ cups dried pitted prunes (1 lb.)

1 cup dried apricots (5½ oz.)

1 cup dried peaches (5½ oz.)

½ cup sugar

3 or 4 slices orange

2 cups water

Rinse fruit in warm water. Drain. Place in a 2 quart baking dish. Add water, sugar and sliced orange. Cover.

Temp: 325°F

Time: 1 Hour

Serves: 6-8

HAM WITH RAISIN SAUCE

2 ham slices ¾″ to 1" thick

¾ cup brown sugar

3 tablespoons cornstarch

1½ teaspoons dry mustard

3 tablespoons vinegar

3 tablespoons lemon juice

½ teaspoon grated lemon rind

2¼ cups water

¾ cups raisins

Trim any skin or excess fat form ham slice. In a saucepan mix brown sugar, cornstarch and dry mustard. Slowly add vinegar. Add lemon juice, lemon rind, water and raisins, cook and stir over medium heat (on top unit control at 225°F) until thickened and clear. Arrange ham slices in single layer in baking pan. Pour sauce over ham.

Temp: 350°F

Time: 1 Hour

Serves: 6-8

PIMIENTO MUSHROOM RICE

1¼ cups converted, long grain rice

1 teaspoon salt

2½ cups boiling water

4 tablespoons butter

2 beef bouillon cubes

1 tablespoon dehydrated onion

1 chopped pimiento

1 small can whole mushrooms

Grease 1½ quart casserole. Add rice, salt, butter, pimiento and mushrooms. Dissolve bouillon cubes in the boiling water and add onion. Pour over rice mixture. Cover tightly with foil.

Temp: 350°F

Time: 1 Hour

Serves: 6-8

SQUASH, MARSHMALLOW, APPLESAUCE CASSEROLE

2 12-ounce packages frozen squash

¼ cup butter

1 teaspoon salt

1 cup applesauce

1 cup miniature marshmallows

Place frozen squash in 1½ quart casserole. Season with the butter and add salt to taste. On top of squash arrange spoonfuls of applesauce. Top with marshmallows.

Temp: 350°F

Time: 1 Hour

Serves: 6-8

EVERYDAY MEAT LOAF

1½ lbs. ground beef

2/3 cup dry bread crumbs

½ cup grated or chopped onion

1 teaspoon salt

½ teaspoon parsley flakes

Dash pepper

2 eggs

1 cup milk

Piquant sauce ingredients:

3 tablespoons brown sugar

1 teaspoon dry mustard

1 teaspoon nutmeg

¼ cup catsup

Combine all ingredients and mix well. Form in one loaf, in a 9 x 5 x 23/4" pan, and cover with Piquant Sauce. Bake.

Piquant sauce:

Combine all ingredients and pour over meat before baking.

Temp: 350°F

Time: 1 Hour 15 Minutes

Serves: 6

SCALLOPED POTATOES

6 medium potatoes

3 tablespoons butter or margarine

4 tablespoons enriched flour

3 cups milk

1 teaspoon salt

¼ teaspoon pepper

2 tablespoons chopped onion

Pare potatoes; Slice thin. Make white sauce by melting butter, add flour and blend to make a paste. Stir in milk a little at a time until well mixed. Put half the potatoes in greased 8" square baking dish; cover with half the sauce, seasonings, and onion, add remaining potatoes, seasonings and onion, then remaining sauce. Bake uncovered.

Temp: 350°F

Time: 1 Hour 15 Minutes

Serves: 6

GLAZED CARROTS

2 No. 303 cans of whole carrots

1 cup brown sugar

3 tablespoons melted butter

¼ cup liquid from carrots

Mix together brown sugar, melted butter and liquid. Pour over carrots in 1½ quart baking dish. Cover. Bake.

Temp: 350°F

Time: 1 Hour 15 Minutes

Serves: 6

MACARONI AND CHEESE

1½ cups macaroni, cooked

2 tablespoons butter

2 tablespoons flour

2 cups milk

½ teaspoon salt

2 teaspoons grated onion

½ pound grated cheddar cheese

¼ cup fine buttered bread crumbs

Paprika

Put cooked macaroni in buttered 1½ quart casserole. Melt butter in sauce pan (on top unit control at 200-212°F). Add flour to butter and blend well. Gradually add milk; stir constantly until smooth. Let cook until sauce boils and thickens to desired consistency. Add salt. Blend onion and cheese with white sauce and pour over cooked macaroni. Sprinkle with buttered crumbs and paprika. Bake uncovered.

Temp: 400°F

Time: 35 Minutes

Serves: 6-8

SAVORY STEWED TOMATOES

2 No. 303 cans (approximately 1 quart) stewed tomatoes

2 tablespoons flour

1 tablespoon sugar

1½ teaspoons salt

¼ teaspoon pepper

1 tablespoon butter

Place tomatoes in a 1½ quart (round) casserole. Add flour, sugar, salt and pepper and mix until well blended. Dot with butter. Bake uncovered.

Temp: 400°F

Time: 35 Minutes

Serves: 6-8

DATE BARS

1 14-ounce package date bar mix

Follow directions for preparing given on the package. Bake.

Temp: 400°F

Time: 35 Minutes

Serves: 6-8

BROILER MEALS

SCOTCH POCKED HAMBURGERS

1 lb. ground beef

1 tsp. salt

1/8 tsp. pepper

2 tsp. Worcestershire sauce

¼ cup finely chopped onion

4 thin slices tomato (medium size)

Mix ground beef with salt and pepper. Flatten beef into large square. Divide into 8 equal parts and make a thin patty of each part. Mix Worcestershire sauce and onion. On half the patties, place a slice of tomato and a tablespoon of chopped onion. Top with second patty and pinch edges together. Place in a shallow pan and broil about 15 minutes, turning once.

Canned white potatoes (or leftover sliced potatoes) may be dipped in melted butter. Sprinkled with seasoning and paprika and placed on broiled pan to heat and brown, after hamburgers are turned.

HALIBUT ALMONDINE

Arrange four Halibut steaks on the broiler rack and brush generously with butter. Broil about 3" to 4" from the heat, about 12 minutes. While fish is broiling, chop fine ½ cup blanched almonds and add to about ¼ cup melted butter. After fish broils, sprinkle crunchy mixture evenly over fish and return to broiler for 1 more minutes. Garnish with lemon and parsley.

BROWN POTATOES-BROILED TOMATOES

Brush leftover or canned white potatoes with melted butter. Sprinkle with paprika. Cut tomatoes in half, sprinkle with buttered bread crumbs and grated cheese. Place on broiler pan and broil with fish for complete broiler meal.

SIX O'CLOCK HAM SWIRLS WITH STUFFED ORANGES

1 lb. ground cooked ham

1 egg

1 tsp. ground cloves

½ cup well drained crushed pineapple

2 cups mashed, seasoned potatoes

2 cups cooked peas

1 can whole kernel corn, cooked

2 tsp. salt

¼ tsp. pepper

2 tbs. Cooking oil

Stuffed oranges

4 medium sized oranges

¼ cup well drained sliced marischino cherries

2 tbsp. honey

Combine ham, egg, cloves and pineapple. Pat out into a rectangle ½" thick on waxed pepper. Spread potatoes evenly over meat, and roll up. Cut into 1 inch slices. Place peas and corn in bottom of broiler pan. Sprinkle with salt, pepper, and cooking oil. Place ham slices on broiler rack. Broil 5 inches form broiler unit for 10 minutes. Cut oranges in half and scoop out pulp. Mix pulp with cherries and fill orange shells. Dribble some honey over each half. Turn meat and place oranges on rack. Continue broiling 8-10 minutes. Serves 8.

CUBE STEAK BROILER DINNER

4 thin cube steaks

Onion salt

Pepper

4 slices Canadian bacon

3 slices Swiss cheese

2 tbsp. Cornflake crumbs

1 tsp. paprika

½ tsp. salt

1 1 lb. can tiny while potatoes, drained

1 tbsp. vegetable liquid or water drained

1 tbsp. instant minced onion

½ tsp. salt

1 16 oz. can green beans, drained

1 3 oz. can chopped mushrooms, drained

1 2 oz. can sliced Pimiento, drained

Sprinkle cube steaks on one side with onion salt and pepper. Place a slice of bacon and cheese on each steak (trim to fit if necessary). Roll from narrow end; secure with toothpicks. Place in center of broiler pan, seam side up.

Combine cornflake crumbs, paprika and salt. Add potatoes and toss gently, until coated. Place potatoes on one side of meat on broiler rack. Broil for 8-10 minutes.

While meat cooks, combinc water and onion. Add salt, beans, mushrooms, and pimiento. Mix gently. Place in aluminium foil "boat".* Turn meat and potatoes. Place beans on pan. Broil 8-10 minutes. Serves 4

* To make foil beat. Have a 12" square of aluminium foil. Fold in half. Crimp ends to form "boat."

BROILED LAMBURGERS

1½ lbs. ground lamb

1½ tsp. salt

1/3 cup milk

Bacon strips

Mix ground lamb with salt and milk. Shape mixtures in five ¾ inch patties. Circle each with a strip of bacon and anchor ends with a toothpick. Score tops.

Paprika potatoes

Drain two 1-pound cans small potatoes. Place in 10 x 7 x 1½ inch foilware pan. Drizzle potatoes with 2 tablespoons melted butter or margarine. (More butter, and salt, pepper and paprika go on when patties are turned).

MINTED PEAR HALVES

Drain canned pear halves. Wait to fill centres with mint jelly till near end of broiling time.

Put beans in broiler pan.

To broil—Arrange the meat patties, potatoes, and pear halves (cut side up) on broiler pan. Broil 4 to 5 inches form heat 12 minutes. Then turn the patties; brush potatoes again with melted butter and season with salt, pepper and paprika. Now broil 5 minutes longer. Fill center of pears with mint jelly. Broil all for another 5 minutes, or till lamb patties are done. Makes 5 servings.

STEAK

Place steak on broiler rack of broiler pan. Place in oven on rack about 3 inches from broiler unit. Turn switch to "Broil". Broil about 10 minutes. Season with salt and pepper. Turn steak and add:

DUTCHESS POTATOES

Season hot mashed potatoes with butter, salt and pepper, add only enough milk to make them fluffy. Add egg yolk; beat well. With tablespoon, drop mounds of potatoes around steak. Shape mounds into nests. Broil until brown about 7 minutes.

Fill potatoes nests with hot cooked peas. Top steak with pat or two of butter. Transfer to platter and serve.

Courtesy: Naigra Mohak Co., USA.

10

Nutrient Guides

NATURE'S PRESCRIPTIONS FOR A HEALTHY HEART

Eat to live, do not live to eat.

Maintain a desirable body weight.

Clean up the oily mess.

Reduce total fat and saturated fat. Avoid cholesterol, and use vegetable oils in moderation.

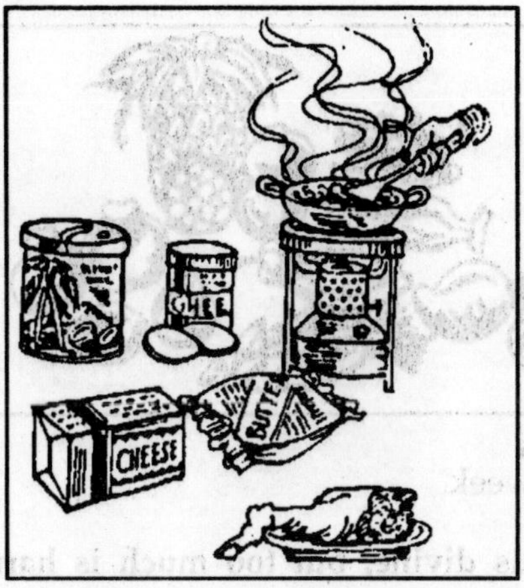

He who follows nature is never out of the way.

Eat natural foods as grown, like coarse grains, whole-grain cereals and pulses, and vegetables. Avoid refined foods, professed foods and sugar.

Nature is bountiful, so stay close to it.

Eat more fresh fruits and vegetables. If you like fish, eat

2-3 times a week.

A little salt is divine, but too much is harmful.

Cut down salt use, eat foods in natural state. Keep the salt intake low.

There is a devil in every berry of the grape.

Avoid alcohol.

Don't get reduced to ashes.

Don't smoke.

The wise depend on exercise for fitness.

Take to regular exercise.

Hope for the best and don't drive yourselves to death.

Get to know the source of your stress. And avoid it. Relax!

NUTRIENT GUIDELINES FOR PREVENTION OF HEART DISEASES

- Calories should be sufficient to maintain appropriate body weight for a given height.
- Total fat intake should be between 15-30% of total calories.

- Cholesterol should not exceed 300 mg/day in the diet. A cholesterol free diet is preferable.
- Saturated fat(s) should be less than 10% of total calories.
- Polyunsaturated fat (P) should not exceed 8% of total calories.
- P/S ratio should be between 0.8-1.0.
- Linoleic acid (LA) should range between 3-7% of calories.
- Alpha-linoleic acid (ALNA) should not be less than 1% of calories.
- La/Alna ratio should be between 5-10.
- Proteins should provide around 10-15% of calories.
- Carbohydrates should constitute 55-65% of calories with emphasis on complex carbohydrates.
- Sugars should be less than 10% of total calories and should be kept to a minimum.
- Slat intake should be between 5-7 g/day.
- Dietary fibre should be round 40 g/day.

A wide variety of foods "As grown" in proper portions should be consumed to provide the necessary carbohydrates, proteins, fats, vitamins, minerals and fibre.

(Guidelines, WHO, 1990).

GUIDE TO A HEALTHY DIET

In order to implement nutrient guidelines, directions are provided for proper food choices in the following tables.

APPROXIMATE CALORIES FROM A GRAM OF RAW FOOD

Food item	Per gram
Cereals 3 kcal	
Pulses	3 kcal
Other vegetables	0.6 kcal
High calorie roots & tubers a	1.0 kcal
Other roots & tubers	0.3 kcal

FOOD GUIDE FOR A HEALTHY HEART

Foods	Prefer	Limit	Avoid
Cereals	wheat, rice, ragi, bajra, maize, jowar and biscuits	foods prepared with maida like white bread	cakes, pastries, naan roti, roomali roti, noodles.
Pulses	whole & sprouted and dhals	-	-
Vegetables	green leafy vegetables and other vegetables	roots and tubers	fried vegetables, banana chips, canned vegetables
Fruits	fresh fruits	syrup.	dried fruits, canned fruits in
Dairy products	low fat milk, buttermilk, skimmed milk	whole milk, milk powders.	Cheese, butter, khoa, condensed milk, milk cream
Eggs	egg white	-	egg yolk
Animal foods	fish	chicken	prawns, shrimps, all types of meat.
Fat	more than one type of vegetable oil	total fat intake	oily dishes, butter, ghee, coconut oil, vanaspati, deep-fired foods

Sugar & sugar products	sugar, jaggery	sugar in any home-made beverages	sweets like chocolates, icecreams.
Nuts & oilseeds		all nuts & oilseeds	
Beverages	fresh fruit juice (without sugar), light tea	coffee, cola, soft drinks	alcohol
Salt	foods in natural state	too much salt in preparations	pickles, papads, sauces, salt biscuits, fried crispies

Food item	Per gram
Green leafy vegetables	0.4 kcal
Milk	0.9 kcal/ml
Skimmed milk	0.3 kcal/ml
Cream	3.0 kcal
Khoa (from whole milk)	4.0 kcal
Cheese	3.5 kcal
Animal foods	1.0 kcal
Spices	3.0 kcal
Sugar	4.0 kcal
Butter	7.0 kcal
Oils/Ghee/Vanaspati	9.0 kcal
Nuts & Oilseeds	6.0 kcal
Eggs	86 kcal/egg

a Sweet potato, potato, colocasia, yam.

For low calorie diets, cut down cereals, fats, cream sugar. Use more vegetables, fruits, pulses, skim milk.

EASY WAY TO COUNT YOUR CALORIES

(Measures providing about 100 K. calories)

Food item	Quantity (g)	Measure (k= katori)
Cereals	30	1/5 K
Millets	30	1/3 K
Pulses	30	¼ K
Leafy vegetables	250	12 bundles
Other vegetables	400	4 K
Roots & Tubers	100	4 K
Nuts & Oilseeds	20	
Fruits	140	One fruit
Milk (buffalo)	90	1/3 K
Milk (cow)	150	1 K
Curd (cow)	170	1 1/6 K

Food item	Quantity (g)	Measure (k= katori)
Buttermilk (lassi)	670	4 K
Cheese	30	1 pkt.
Ghee	10	2 tsp.
Butter	15	3 tsp.
Egg	60	-
Chicken	90	-
Mutton	85	-
Fish (lean)	100	-
Fish (fatty)	60	-
Shrimps	30	-
Prawns	100	-
Sugar	25	5 tsp.
Vegetables oils and vanaspati	10	2 tsp.
Spices	40	6 tsp.

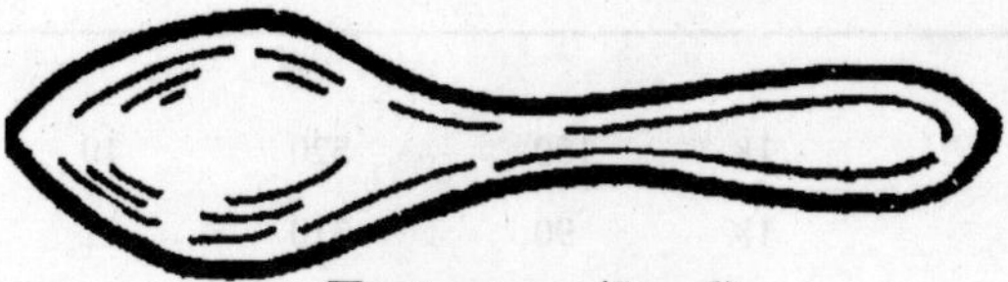

Teaspoon (5 ml)

Tablespoon (15 ml)

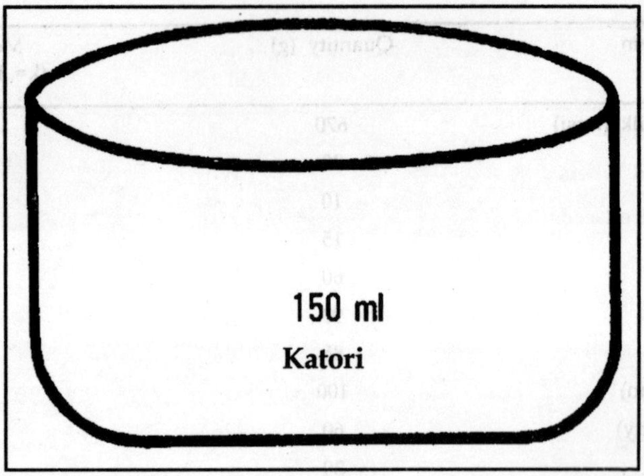

CALORIES, PROTEIN AND FAT CONTENT OF COMMON FOOD ITEMS (RAW) (HOUSEHOLD MEASURES)

Item	Measure	Weight g.	Energy Kcal.	Protein g.	Fat g.
Cereals					
Rice	1K	150	520	10	3
Wheat flour	1K	90	310	11	3
Millet flour	1K	90	300	11	3
Pulses					
Bengalgram dhal	1K	130	485	27	9
Other dhals	1K	135	460	32	3
Whole pulses					
Green gram	1K	140	470	34	3
Cowpea (lobia)	1K	135	440	33	4
Rajmah	1K	120	415	27	3
Soyabean	1K	130	530	60	27
Green leafy vegetables	5 B	100	62	3.0	0.4

Item	Measure	Weight g.	Energy Kcal.	Protein g.	Fat g.
Other vegetables		100	26	2.0	0.2
Roots and tubers		100	105	1.0	1.0
Nuts and oilseeds					
Almonds	10 No.	15	85	3.0	8
Cashewnuts	10No.	15	95	3.0	8
Coconut (fresh)	1 No.	115	510	5.0	50
Coconut (dry)	½ No.	45	290	3.0	30
Groundnuts	50 No.	15	85	4.0	6
Sesame seeds	1tsp.	3	15	0.6	1
Spices					
Chillie powder	1 tsp.	7	17	1.0	1.0
Coriander seeds	1 tsp.	7	20	1.0	1.4
Cumin seeds	1 tsp.	5	18	1.0	0.5
Fenugreek	1 tsp.	6	20	1.6	0.6
Mustard seeds	1 tsp.	10	5	2.0	4.0
Garlic	6 pods.	3	4	0.2	0.02
Onion	1 med.	50	30	0.9	0.1
Animal foods					
Milk (Buffalo)	1 K	150 ml.	175	6.0	10
Milk (cow)	1 K	150 ml.	100	5.0	6
Egg (hen)	One	60	100	8.0	8.0
Mutton		100	194	18.0	13.3
Fish (lean)		100	100	18.0	1.5
Fish (fatty)		100	150	90.0	6.0

B: Bundles K: Katori tsp: teaspoon.

Soucre: Gopalan *et al.*, 1989; Ghafoorunissa, 1989a; Pasricha, 1989.

APPROXIMATE NUTRIENT VALUE OF COMMON COOKED FOODS

Item	No. of serving	Weight of cooked preparation g.	Energy Kcal	Fat g.	Protein g.
1. Cereal preparations					
Rice	1K	100	110	0.1	2
Idli	1	60	75	0.1	2
Plain dosa	1	40	125	3	3
Masala dosa	1	100	200	6	4
Phulka	1	35	80	0	3
Paratha	1	50	150	4	4
Upma	1K	130	200	9	5
Sevian upma	1K	80	130	4	3
Bread toasted	2 slices	50	170	1	4
Poha (Awal)	1K	100	200	9	2
Dhalia	1K	140	165	7	5
Kichidi	1K	100	210	7	4
Puri	1	25	80	3	2
II. Pulse preparations					
Plain dhal	1K	140	170	4	10
Sambar	1K	160	81	2	4
Chole/Sundal	1K	150	115	5	7
III. Vegetable preparations					
With gravy	1K	130	130	7	3
Dry	1K	100	115	7	2
Bagara Baigan	1K	170	230	20	3
Vegetable kofta	1K	145	220	14	4
IV. Fried snacks					
Bhajji	1	7	35	3	0.5
Samosa	1	65	210	12	2
Kachori	1	45	200	12	3

Item	No. of serving	Weight of cooked preparation g.	Energy Kcal	Fat g.	Protein g.
Potato Bonda	1	40	100	5	3
Sago vada	1	30	100	6	1
Masala vada	1	20	56	2	2
Vada	1	20	65	3	3
Dahi vada	1	80	170	9	5
Vegetable cutlet	1	30	70	5	1
V. Chutneys					
Coconut/ground nuts/til/coriander	1tbsp	25	64	5	3
Tomato	1tbsp	20	10	0.3	0.3
VI. Non-Vegetarian preparations					
Boiled egg	1	50	86	7.0	7.0
Omlette	1	65	155	14.0	7.0
Fried egg	1	50	155	14.0	7.0
Mutton curry	1K	145	240	18	10
Chicken curry	1K	125	260	15	26
Fish (fried)	2pieces	85	220	12	18
VII. Bakery products					
Biscuits	2	40	220	14	3
Cake	1	40	220	13	3
Vegetable puff	1	60	170	10	3
VIII. Sweets					
Laddu, burfi etc.	1	60	250	15	8
Halwa (sjui)	1K	130	430	20	3
Double ka meetha	1K	105	280	18	4
Custard/puddings	1K	110	180	6	5
Chikki	2	60	300	12	8
Jam/Jelly	1tsp.	7	20	0.04	0.04

K = Katori, tbsp = tablespoon, tsp = teaspoon.
Calories and fat will depend on sugar and oil/ghee added.
Source: Pasricha, 1989.

SALADS AND CALORIES

Item	No. (Medium size)	Weight	K.cals.
Beetroot	1	65	30
Cabbage	1	250	70
Carrot	1	40	20
Cucumber	1	90	12
Lettuce	6 bundles	100	20
Onion	1	50	25
Radish	1	60	10
Tomato	1	50	10
Turnip	1	100	30

Note: You can exchange salads freely for any other item of the food to fill your stomach and lower your calorie intake.
Approximately 300-400 g. of a salad combination carries 100 calories.
Wash vegetables thoroughly and use either raw or after a short exposure to steam in pressure cooker.

FRUITS AND CALORIES

Item	No./Quantity	Weight (g.)	K.cals.
Apple	1	100	65
Banana	1	80	90
Grapes	30	100	70
Guava	1	100	50
Jack fruit	4 pieces	100	90
Mango	1	250	180
Mosambi/orange	1	100	40
Papaya	1peice	250	80
Pineapple	1piece	100	50
Sapota	1	80	80
Custard apple	1	130	130
Watermelon/muskmelon	1piece	100	15

One banana is equal in terms of calories to two apples or two guavas or two mosambis or 8 pieces of watermelon.

A mango is equal in terms of calories to 3 apples.

BEVERAGES AND CALORIES

Item	Measure	Quantity (ml)	K.cals.
Coffee	1cup	150	100
Tea	1cup	50	60
Carbonated beverages	1bottle	200	150
Fresh lime juice	1glass	200	60
Squash	1glass	200	80
Syrups (shrebat)	1glass	200	200

DIET PROVIDING 1000 KCALS WITH FOODS WHICH ARE KNOWN TO BE PROTECTIVE FOR HEART DISEASE

Foods	Vegetarian g.	Non-vegetarian g.
Cereals	140	140
Pulses	40	30
Green leafy vegetables	100	100
Other vegetables	150	1504
Roots and tubers	100	100
Fruits	100	100
Milk (low fat)	200	200
Oil	15	15
Flesh foods	-	50
Fish	-	100 (fatty) or 200 (lean)
Egg (white only)		1
NUTRIENTS		
Protein		38 g.
Carbohydrates		156 g.
Fat		22 g.
Saturated fatty acids		4 g.
Fibre		35 g.

Linoleic acid	7 g.
Alpha-linolenic acid	1 g.
Carotene	4000 ug.
Cholesterol	<50 mg.
Calcium	800 mg.
Riboflavin	0.9 mg.
Thiamin	0.9 mg.
Vitamin C	135 mg.

- Flesh foods (mutton/chicken) not more than once a week.
- Fish : 2-3 times/week.
- Egg yolk to be avoided, but egg which can be taken.
- Condiments and spices to suit your taste.
- Daily usage of the following offers an additional advantage;

Garlic 0.5 g, methi seeds 5 g. (one tsp), methi can be included in various preparations to one's taste and choice (phulkas, idlis, sambar, dosa, etc.)

SAMPLE MENU FOR 1000 KCALS DIET: VEGETARIAN

Early Morning	Tea/Coffee	One cup	
Breakfast	Phulkas	Two	
	Dhal curry	3 tbsp	300 Kcals
	Tea/Coffee	One cup	
Mid morning	Any fruit	One	
Lunch	Rice	1 Katori	
	Dhal with any green Leafy vegetable	1 Katori	
	Rasam or Vegetable Soup	1 Katori	400 Kcals
	Buttermilk	1 Katori	
	Salad of tomato Onion, carrot	1 each	
Snack	Upma	1 Katori	

Tea	Tea/Coffee	1 cup	
Dinner	Rice	1 Katori	
	Any vegetable curry	1 Katori	
	Rasam	1 Katori	
	Buttermilk	1 Katori	300 Kcals
	Salad of carrot, radish		
	Cucumber	1 each	
Bedtime	Any fruit	One	

- A multivitamin pill with B-complex and several minerals, containing about 5 times the recommended dietary allowances (Tables 6a and 6b) should be taken once in a day on reducing diets.
- Tea/Coffee to be taken without sugar.
- Cooking oil not to exceed 15 g.

BREAKFAST EXCHANGES

Paratha with	....	One
Potato curry	....	½ Katori
Puri	...	Two
Potato curry	....	½ Katori
Idli	....	Two
Coconut chutney	....	1 tbsp
Or Sambar	.....	¾ Katori
Vada	....	Two
Sambar	....	1 Katori
Dosa	....	Two
Coconut chutney	....	1 tbsp

SNACK EXCHANGES

Poha	....	½ Katori
Bhajji	....	3
Masala vada	....	2
Potato Bonda	....	1
Sago vada	....	1

Sandwich	....	1
Savian upma	....	¾ K
Puffed rice	....	½ K
Salt biscuits	....	2 Nos.
Sweet biscuits	....	2 Nos.
Plain cake (50 g.)	....	¾
Chole	....	¾ K
Sundal	....	¾ K

LUNCH EXCHANGES

Rice		Dhal	
Pulao	¾ K	Raita with onions	½ K
Kichidi	½ K	Sambar	1 K
Lime rice	¾ K	Green vegetable Kootu	¾ K
Tamarind rice	¾ K	Kadi	¾ K

DINNER EXCHANGES

Rice-1 Katori Or Phulka-2	Vegetable		Rasam	
	Peas + Panir	½ K	Tamarind rasam	1K
	Potato curry	½ K	Carrot soup	½ K
	Vegetable kofta curry	½ K	Tomato soup	½ K
	Vegetable kurma	¾ K	Mixed vegetable soup	½ K
	Beans curry	1 K		
	Capsicum curry	3/4 K		
	Cauliflower & Carrot curry	1 K		
	Kovai curry	1¼ K		
	Lady's finger curry	¾ K		
	Ridge gourd curry	1 K		
	Stuffed tomato	1 No.		
	Dam-ka-chicken	½ K		
	Fish cutlet	1		
	Fish fry	1 big piece		
	Prawns curry	½ K		
	Mutton curry	½ K		

K = Katori.

For recipes, refer Pasricha, 1989.

The exchanges ensure selection of a wide variety of food items and permits one to eat the same foods as the rest of the family members.

Remember that the visible fat employed should not exceed 15 g/1000 Kcals.

The exchanges given above are equivalent to sample menu items only in terms of calories.

PLANNING YOUR DIET

Objectives

To reduce body weight and to control blood cholesterol and blood glucose without losing the protective nutrients.

Steps

1. Consult your doctor or dietitian to fix the desirable calorie intake.
2. Draw up a list of all the food items you consume in a typical day.
3. Use Table 21 to assess whether your current intake of total calories, fat and protein falls within the recommended range.
4. If your present intake of total calories, fat, protein and fibre falls within the range recommended for YOU and if you are also consuming fresh fruits and vegetables daily, CONGRATULATIONS! You are taking a balanced diet and there is no need to exchange your dietary habits.
5. If, however, your present intake differs from the recommendations, adjust your diet accordingly.
6. For example, if you are advised 1000 Kcals (Table 25) look up the tables giving food quantities and calories (Tables 18 to 20).
7. Keep your protein intake at 35 g. (15% of total calories).

8. Keep your fat intake (visible + invisible) around 20 g. (20% of total calories).
9. Remember that you are getting about 8 g. of invisible fat from food items, such as cereals, pulses, milk, meat, etc. (table 7). Therefore, the rest can be visible fat. Avoid saturated fat and cholesterol (Tables 8 and 9).
10. Use any vegetable oil except coconut and vanaspati along with mustard oil (Table 8).
11. Choose n-3 PUFA, fibre and antioxidant rich foods (Tables 10-12). You will then get everything you need.

SIMPLE MESSAGES

Tips for good eating

- Make breakfast the largest and dinner the lightest meal of the day.
- Be a nibbler, not a gourmet.
- Eat your salad before you eat the meal.
- Don't starve yourself and overeat subsequently.
- Before cooking, remove all fat from meats and also skin from chicken.
- Avoid purchasing minced meat, the butcher finds it more profitable to sell this without removing fat surrounding the flesh portion.
- Do not sieve wheat and millet flours as it reduces the nutrients and fibre.
- Repeated heating of oils should be avoided.
- Use a scrubber and not a peeler for removing the skin from vegetables.
- Avoid deep frying and prefer steamed foods.
- Use non-stick pans and vessels to cut down the use of cooking oil.
- Fast foods and canned foods are costly, both for your pocket and your heart.
- Don't overuse salt.

- Dine at least two hours before you go to bed.
- Yellow, orange and green vegetables and fruits add life to your heart.
- Remember that heat, light and air are enemies of anti-oxidant vitamins. Don't cut vegetables and expose them to light for long periods, pressure cook the vegetables.
- As age advances, eat less, exercise more.

Eating on time, a variety of natural plant foods with low fat milk and less salt, in quantities to maintain ideal weight is the key to a healthy long life.

POINTS TO PONDER

1. A cup of tea with 2 tsp sugar 5 times a day provides you the maximum permissible sugar.
2. A medium-sized sweet item of any type gives calories equivalent to 50 g. raw rice.
3. Three cups of milk give 10 g. of saturated fat, 1/3rd the suggested upper limit of saturated fat for diets providing 2400 Kcals.
4. About 2 tsp of butter or ghee per day gives about 1/4th the suggested upper limit of saturated fat for diets providing 2400 Kcals.
5. A regular consumption of legumes/dhals (particularly blackgram/rajmah/lobia) and green leafy vegetables, fenugreek and mustard seeds adds to the quality of fat in Indian diets.
6. Fish improves the quality of fat.
7. One egg provides 210 mg. of cholesterol.
8. One tsp of pickle gives about 1.5 g. of salt and about 2 g. of fat, 1 papad gives about 0.5 g. of salt.
9. Though nuts such as almonds, cashewnuts and walnuts have high levels of monounsaturated fatty acids which are not harmful like saturated fatty acids, these nuts have to be limited/avoided because of their high fat content. 5 almonds gives about 1 tsp fat.

FALLACIES AND FACTS

	Fallacies		Facts
1.	A zero fat diet is excellent.	No	Some amount of fat is necessary.
2.	Cholesterol containing foods are the only culprits.	No	Saturated fats also increase blood cholesterol. The two together have additive effects.
3.	Only oils need to be cut down.	No	A total change to a healthy dietary lifestyle is also necessary.
4.	Plenty of vegetable oils are good.	No	Moderation in their use must be exercised.
5.	Safflower and sunflower oils can be taken as much as you want.	No	Excess of these oils can decrease "good" cholesterol.
6.	Vegetable oils do not have cholesterol.	Yes	But vegetable oils consumed in excess can cause an increase in total fat intake. Too much of fat in the diet increases blood cholesterol.
7.	Starvation and rapid decrease in body weight are good.	No	Body weight reduction should be gradual, starvation is not the solution.

8.	One meal a day is good for body weight reduction.	No	Frequent and small meals are far better.
9.	Alcohol is good for the heart.	No	Alcohol does not increase "good" cholesterol.
10.	Only plain sugars increase blood sugar levels.	No	All carbohydrates can increase blood sugar, refined foods and sugar increase blood glucose rapidly.
11.	Only fat people need to worry.	No	Even individuals who are normal in weight can have higher body fat and blood lipids.
12.	Only vigorous exercises are good.	No	Even a long brisk walk will help very much.

11

Cooking of Hospital Diets

INTRODUCTION

It is true that each patient requires individual attention about his diet. His food preferences and his nutrient requirements have to be carefully considered. A set of standard therapeutic diets can be used as a guide for prescribing or formulating a diet. This brochure contains a few such diets.

The Nutrition Expert Group has recommended balanced diets suitable for normal adult males weighing about 55 kg. The therapeutic diets described here are appropriate modifications of this balanced diet. Only the quantities of foodstuffs to be used are given here. The menus may be planned according to the usual dietary pattern of the individual patient to ensure maximum acceptability of the modified diet.

Peptic ulcer and diabetic patients require a specific pattern of distribution of the nutrients and hence the menus for such diets are also included in this brochure.

The foodstuffs can be cooked according to the method the patient is used to. The amount of oil or ghee mentioned in the diets, is to be used for cooking purposes.

In the appendix, an exchange list is given. It can be used to ensure variety in the diet and to formulate new diets.

The foods which must be strictly avoided by different patients are given along with each modified diet.

The nutritive value of all the foodstuffs except the sodium content of skimmed milk powder has been calculated using values given in the book "Nutritive Value of Indian Foods' (1985) brought out by this Institute. The sodium content of skimmed milk powder was calculated according to the values given by Bills et al., in the Journal of American Dietetic Association (25 : 304, 1949).

Volume of one katori used to measure the food is 150 ml.

Recommended dietary allowances for a male sedentary worker*

Net calories	2400 Kcal
Proteins	55 g
Calcium	0.4-0.5 g
Iron	24 mg
Vitamin A	
Retinol or	750 ug
Carotene	3000 ug
Thiamin	1.2 mg
Riboflavin	1.4 mg
Nicotinic acid	16 mg
Vitamin B6	2.0 mg
Ascorbic acid	40 mg
Folic acid	100 μg
Vitamins B_{12}	1 μg

*As recommended by the ICMR in 1981.

The diets contained in this booklet have been computed keeping in view these recommended allowances.

FULL DIET

This is a normal diet which is modified from the balanced a recommended by ICMR. It provides all the nutrients in slightly high amounts than recommended for a healthy male sedentary worker. It can be used for an adult patient (male or female) admitted in a hospital who does not need any dietary modification.

This is also known as general or regular diet.

Principle

The following foods should be avoided while formulating the:

1. All bran, coarse cereals
2. Too much of spices and condiments
3. Fried foods

Sample diet

Foodstuff	Vegetarian g	Non-vegetarian g
Cereals	400	400
Pulses	70	50
Green leafy vegetables	50	50
Other vegetables	100	100
Roots and tubers	100	100
Fruits	100	100
Milk	400	200
Flesh foods	-	100
Sugar	20	20
Oil (for cooking)	20	30

This diet provides

Calories	2450
Proteins	77 g
Calcium	1.1 g
Iron	43 µg
Retinol	800 mg
Thiamin	1.9 mg
Riboflavin	1.4 mg

Distribution

Cooked measures

In different meals	East India	West India	North India	South India
Bed tea (6 am)	Tea 1 cup	Coffee 1 cup	Tea 1 cup	Coffee 1 cup
Breakfast (8-9am)				
Bread	6 slices	-	6 slices	-
Butter	1 tsp.	-	1tsp.	-
Idli	-	4	-	4
Chutney	-	2 tbsp	-	2 tbsp
Milk with sugar	1 cup	1 cup	1 cup	1 cup
Lunch (12 noon-1 pm)				
Rice	4 K	2 K	-	4 K
Chapattis	-	3	5	-
Dal	1¾ K	3¾ K	1½ K	-
Sambar	-	-	-	1 K
Green leafy vegetable with potato	1 K	1 K	1 K	1 K
Salad	1 cucumber with ½ lime	One	1 cucumber with ½ lime	1 tomato
Curd	1 K sweet	½ K	1 K	½ K
Orange or sweet lime	One	One	One	One

In different meals	East India	West India	North India	South India
Dinner (6-7 pm)				
Rice	4 K	2 K	-	4 K
Chapati	-	3	5	-
Dal	$1^1/_3$ katori	¾ K	1½ K	1 K
Sambar	-	-	-	1 K
Rasam	-	-	-	1 K
Other vegetables with onions	1 K	1 K	1 K	1 katori
Curd	-	½ K	-	½ K

K = katori.

Non-vegetarians can include:

1. Eggs two or mutton or fish curry 1 katori
2. Use 3 tsp. of extra oil to cook and cut down 1 cup of milk and dal for one meal

HALF DIET

This diet provides the nutrients required for children, upto the age of 10 years. It is a normal diet which is modified from the balanced diet recommended for children, by ICMR. It can be used for children who do not need any specific diet. This is also known as children's diet.

Principle

The following foods should be avoided while formulating the diet.

1. All bran, coarse cereals
2. Too much of spices and condiments
3. Fried foods

Sample diet

Foodstuffs	Vegetarian g	Non-vegetarian g
Cereals	225	225
Pulses	60	40
Green leafy vegetables	25	25
Other vegetables	75	75
Roots and tubers	75	75
Fruits	100	100
Milk	400 ml	300 ml
Meat/fish/egg	-	50
Sugar	30	30
Oil (for cooking)	20	25

This diet provides

Calories	1800
Proteins	55 g
Calcium	972 mg
Iron	26 mg
Retinol	520 μg
Thiamin	1.3 mg
Riboflavin	1.1 mg

Distribution of the diet can be done as fro full diet.

KHICHERI DIET

It is a soft diet which provides most of the nutrients required by a male adult. It is slightly deficient in iron, calories and riboflavin. It is a transitional diet between the liquid diet and full diet.

Sample diet

Foodstuffs	Amount (g)
Rice	200
Green gram dal or lentil dal	70
Calabash cucumber or Ridge gourd	100
Potatoes and Onions	100
Orange or Sweet lime or Banana	200
Milk	400 ml
Eggs or	Two
Paneer or Cheese	50
Sugar	30
Oil (to cook)	20

This diet provides

Calories	2000
Proteins	64 g
Calcium	890 mg
Iron	19.5 mg
Retinol	785 μg
Thiamin	1.4 mg
Riboflavin	1.1 mg

MILK AND BREAD DIET

This is also a soft diet which provides all nutrients expect calories, iron and thiamin in the amounts required for an adult man. It is also a transitional diet between the liquid and full diet. It can be used for the patients who do not like khicheri diet.

Sample diet

Foodstuff	Amount
Milk	1000 ml
Bread	100 g
Potato	200 g
Banana or orange	200 g
Eggs or	Two
Paneer or cheese	50 g
Sugar	50 g
Butter	30 g

This diet provides

Calories	2000
Protein	62 g
Calcium	1810 mg
Iron	8.4 mg
Retinol	1504 ug
Thiamin	1.1 mg
Riboflavin	1.7 mg

LIQUID DIET

This diet is designed to give oral nourishment in the liquid form. It can be used for the patients who cannot tolerate or consume solid or semi-solid foods. Since this diet does not provide enough nutrients it should not be continued for more than necessary time.

Sample diet

Foodstuff	*Amount*
Milk	1000 ml
Fruit juice	1000 ml

Eggs	Two
Sugar	50 g

This diet provides

Calories	1400
Protein	52 g
Calcium	1760 mg
Iron	11.1 mg
Retinol	1100 ug
Thiamin	1.4 mg
Riboflavin	1.8 mg

DIET FOR PREGNANT WOMAN

This diet provides slightly higher amounts of protein, calories, minerals and vitamins than required for a normal woman. It can be given to a pregnant woman in the second and third trimester of pregnancy when there is extra demand for these nutrients because of the developing fetus.

Principle

All the foodstuffs available to the family can be taken by a pregnant woman. There is no specific taboo on any foodstuff.

Sample diet

Foodstuff	Sedentary work Vegetarian g	Moderate work Vegetarian g
Cereals	445	475
Pulses	55	60
Green leafy vegetables	100	100
Other vegetables	40	40
Roots and tubers	50	50

Milk	200 ml	250 ml
Fats and oils	20	20
Sugar and jaggery	30	30

This diet provides about

Calories	2200	2500
Proteins (g)	70	75
Fat (g)	40	50

Non-vegetarians can substitute the pulses with 2 eggs or 50 g of meat or fish, plus 10 g of fat.

DIET FOR NURSING WOMAN

This diet provides slightly more of all nutrients than what are required by a normal woman. It can be used by a nursing mother, throughout her lactation period.

All the foodstuffs available can be consumed by a lactating mother. There is no specific taboo on any foodstuff.

Sample diet

Foodstuff	Sedentary work Vegetarian g	Moderate work Vegetarian g
Cereals	470	500
Pulses	70	75
Green leafy vegetables	100	100
Other vegetables	40	40
Roots and tubers	50	50
Milk	200 ml	250 ml
Fats and oils	30	35
Sugar and jaggery	30	30

This diet provides about

Calories	2450	2750
Proteins (g)	75	80
Fat (g)	50	60

Non-vegetarians can substitute pulses with 2 eggs or 50 g of meat or fish, plus 10 g of fat.

BLAND DIET

A bland diet is a diet which is non-irritating chemically and mechanically and which inhibits gastric secretion. It can be used for gastric and duodenal ulcer patients after acute symptoms have subsided. With slight changes and reduction in fibre and fat content it can also be used for diarrhea and ulcerative colitis.

Principle

The following foods should be avoided while formulating the diet:

1. All bran, coarse cereals
2. Skin and seeds of fruits
3. Raw vegetables
4. Vegetables like cabbage, beans, ladies-fingers and bitter gourd etc.
5. Spices and condiments
6. Fried foods
7. Strong beverages
8. Pickles, chutneys etc.
9. Tender coconut water
10. Chocolates, pudding and similar preparations
11. Meat extracts and soups

Sample diet

Foodstuffs	*Vegetarian*
Rice	100 g
White bread	40 g
Pulses	40 g
Potatoes	75 g
Vegetables	100 g
Milk	1000 ml
Curd	300 g
Skimmed milk powder	15 g
Orange juice	150 g
Banana	50 g
Sugar	25 g
Butter	7 g
Ghee or oil	25 g

Note: Non-vegetarians can take a half-boiled egg instead of skimmed milk powder.
*This amount can be used for cooking purposes.

This diet provides

Calories	2000
Protein	75 g
Fat	90 g
Carbohydrates	220 g

Distribution

Cooked measures		**Cooked measures**	
7 A.M.		**1 P.M.**	
Milk	1 glass	Soft boiled rice	2 katories
Sugar	1 tsp	Sieved cauliflower and carrots	1½ katori

Half boiled egg	1	curd	1 katori
Or			
Skimmed milk powder to Be mixed with milk	3 tsp	sieved green gram dal (dehusked)	¼ katori
10 A.M.		**4 P.M.**	
Toast	Two	Milk	1 glass
Butter	1 tsp	Sugar	1 tsp.
Milk	1 glass	Biscuits	Two
Sugar	1 tsp	Banana	Half
7 P.M.		**10 P.M.**	
Soft boiled rice	2 katories	Milk	1 glass
Sieved lentil dal	¼ katori	Sugar	1 tsp
Mashed potato	½ katori		
Curd	1 katori		
Sieved orange juice	½ glass		

DIABETIC DIET

This diet is as close to the normal diet as possible so as to meet the nutritional needs and the treatment of the individual patient. This diet is slightly low in carbohydrates, but adequate in other food principles.

Principle

The following foods should be avoided in all diabetic diets:

1. Roots and tubers
2. Sweets, puddings and chocolates
3. Fried foods
4. Dried fruits and nuts
5. Sugar
6. Fruits like banana, sapota, custardapple etc.

Sample diet

Foodstuffs	*Vegetation (g)*	*Non-Vegetarian (g)*
Cereals	200	250
Pulses	60	20
Green leafy vegetables	200	200
Other vegetables	200	200
Fruits	200	200
Milk (dairy)	400	200
Oil	20	20
Fish/chicken without skin	-	100

This diet provides

Calories	1600
Protein	65 g
Fat	40 g
Carbohydrates	245 g

Distribution

	Cooked measures	
	Vegetarian	Non-vegetarian
Bed tea		
Coffee or tea	1 cup	1 cup
Breakfast		
Toast with a little butter	1	1
Coffee or tea	1 cup	1 cup
Lunch		
Rice	2 katories	2 katories
Sambar	1 katori	1 katori
Green leafy vegetable	1 katori	1 katori

Curd	½ katori	½ katori
Tomato or citrus fruit	1	1
Pickle	a piece	a piece
Tea		
Tea or coffee	1 cup	1 cup
Upma	¾ katori	1 katori
Dinner		
Phulka (chapatti)	3	4
Dal	1 katori	-
Curd	½ katori	-
Fish/chicken	-	2 pieces
Other vegetables with gravy	1 katori	1 katori
Roasted papad	1	1
Tomato or cucumber	1	1
Before going to bed		
Milk	1 cup	1 cup

Note: 5 tsp. of oil can be used in cooking

LOW-CALORIE DIET

The diet provides less calories than the total energy requirements for the day; thus it provides for depletion of body fat. It is used in cases of obesity, cardiac disturbances and hypertension in over-weight individuals.

Principle

The following foods should be avoided while formulating the diet:

1. Sweets, chocolates, jaggery, jam, honey, preserves, puddings, cakes etc.
2. Roots and tubers
3. Fried foods

4. Dried fruits and nuts
5. Alcoholic drinks and soft drinks unless they contain artificial sweetening agents instead of sugar
6. Cream and free fats
7. Fruits like banana, custard-apple, sapota, dates etc.

Sample diet

Foodstuffs	Vegetarian (g)	Non-vegetarian (g)
Wheat flour	60	60
Rice	30	60
Other vegetables	200	200
Green leafy vegetables	200	200
Pulses	70	50
Citrus fruit or tomato	200	200
Milk (cow's)	600 ml	250 ml
Skimmed milk powder	20	-
Oil or ghee	7	12
Lean meat or fish	-	50
Egg	-	One

This diet provides

Calories	1200
Protein	60 g
Fat	30 g
Carbohydrates	170 g

HIGH-CALORIE DIET

This is a normal diet supplemented with high calorie foods so that the bulk of the diet is not much increased. It can be used for fevers, convalescence after prolonged illness, leanness and hyperthyroidism.

Principle

The following foods should be avoided if the patient is convalescing or having fever.

1. Fried foods
2. Dry fruits and nuts

Sample diet

Foodstuffs	Weight of raw ingredients	
	Vegetarian (g)	Non-vegetarian (g)
Cereals	250	300
Pulses	100	50
Roots and tubers	50	75
Other vegetables	50	50
Green leafy vegetables	100	100
Bread	60	60
Butter	10	20
Milk	750 ml	300 ml
Curd	100	-
Sugar	50	50
Ghee or oil	30	30
Banana	150	250
Egg	-	One
Meat or fish	-	100

This diet provides

Calories	2700
Proteins	80 g
Fat	70 g

LOW FAT DIET

This is a normal diet modified to reduce the fat content to approximately 30 g per day. It may be used in treating diseases with intolerance to fat such as gall bladder, liver and pancreatic diseases or in conditions of steatorrhoea.

Principle

The following foods should be avoided in such diets:

1. High fat foods like nuts, cheese etc.
2. Fried foods
3. Free fat and cream etc.

Sample diet

Foodstuffs	Vegetarian (g)	Non-vegetarian (g)
Cereals	200	250
Pulses	100	75
Cow's milk	-	100 ml
Skimmed milk powder	50	-
Curd (Cow's milk)	200	-
Green leafy vegetables	100	100
Other vegetables	100	100
Potatoes	50	50
Sugar	50	50
Banana	75	75
Orange	100	100
Ghee or oil to cook	17	15
Chicken or fish	-	100
Eggs	-	One

This diet provides

Calories	2100
Protein	75 g
Fat	30 g
Carbohydrates	385 g

GLUTEN FREE DIET

This diet is as close to the normal diet as possible. So as to meet the nutritional needs of the patient suffering from Coeliac diseases, it can also be used for patients with gluten-induced enteropathy and dermatitis herpetiformis. The calories can be adjusted to the requirement of the patient.

Principle

The following foods should be avoided in gluten free diets:

1. Wheat & Wheat products like flour, whiteflour, semolina and dahlia (broken wheat).
2. Bread, cake, pastries, biscuits and nan etc.

Sample diet

Foodstuffs	Vegetarian (g)	Non-vegetarian (g)
Rice	300	300
Sago	50	75
Corn flakes	25	25
Pulses	75	30
Green leafy vegetables	50	50
Other vegetables	100	100
Roots and tubers	100	100
Fruits	100	100

Milk	300	100
Sugar	30	30
Fats and oils	30	30
Flesh foods	-	100

This diet provides

Calories	2400
Protein	60 g
Fat	50 g

LOW CHOLESTEROL AND REDUCED SATURATED FAT DIET

This is a normal diet formulated with increased polyunsaturated fats. It is adequate in all nutrients. It can help to lower plasma cholesterol, calories and protein can be changed with individual needs.

Principle

The following foods should be avoided while formulating the diet:

1. Butter, hydrogenated fat, and lard
2. Coconut and coconut oil
3. Foods cooked with these fats
4. Fatty meat, visible fat on meat sausages etc.
5. Whole milk and cream
6. Chocolate and ice cream
7. Cheese
8. Organ meats like liver, kidney and brain etc.
9. Shrimp
10. Eggs only two per week

Sample diet

Foodstuffs	Amounts (g)
Cereals	300
Pulses	50
Green leafy vegetables	50
Other vegetables	100
Roots and tubers	100
Fruits	100
Skimmed milk	400
Sugar	30
Oil	30

THIS DIET PROVIDES

Calories	2400
Protein	70 g
Fat	55 g
Carbohydrates	400 g

LOW SODIUM DIET

This is a normal diet but with a low sodium content. The food preparations for this diet are cooked without extra salt and high sodium foods are avoided. This is designed for use in conditions where there is sodium retention like oedema, nephritis, cardiac diseases, toxaemia of pregnancy and hypertension.

Principle

The following foods should be avoided while formulating the diet:

1. Salt in cooking or on table

2. Sea fish, salted meat and salted dry fish, liver etc.
3. Salted butter and cheese
4. All foods to which salt or baking soda has been added in cooking
5. Pickles and chutneys

Sample diet

Foodstuffs	Vegetarian (g)	Non-vegetarian (g)
Rice	250	300
Dal	100	75
Fruits	200	200
Vegetables	200	200
Potatoes	100	125
Milk (Cow's)	600 ml	200 ml
Oil	30	30
Sugar	30	50
Meat or fish	-	50
Eggs	-	One

This diet provides

Calories	2200
Protein	70 g
Sodium (as sodium)	0.5 g

LOW OXALIC ACID DIET

This is a normal diet with a low oxalic acid content. High oxalic acid foods are avoided. This is designed for use by the patients suffering from oxalate calculi.

Principle

Foods rich in oxalic acid should be avoided while formulating the diet.

Sample diet

Foodstuffs	Vegetarian (g)	Non-vegetarian (g)
Rice	200	200
Wheat flour	200	200
Red gram dal	50	35
Black gram dal	20	20
Cabbage	100	100
Potato	75	75
Mango	75	75
Milk	200 ml	100 ml
Oil	35	40
Sugar	30	30
Mutton or Rohu fish	-	30
Egg	-	30

This diet provides

Calories	2400
Protein	65 g
Fat	50 g
Carbohydrates	425 g

LOW PURINE, LOW FAT DIET

This is a rater restricted diet. It provides low purine and low fat, hence can be deficient in some nutrients like certain 'B' vitamins and iron if care is not exercised in menu planning. It is designed to be used for gout and gouty arthritis patients.

Principles

The following foods should be avoided while formulating the diet.

1. Sweet breads, anchovies, sardines, liver, kidney, brain pancreas, bacon, beef, lamb, prok, meat, extracts and gravies.
2. Dried beans, peas and lentils
3. Mushroom, cauliflower and spinach
4. Alcoholic beverages, chocolate, cocoa, tea and coffee except as specified.

Sample diet

Foodstuffs	Quantity (g)
Rice or atta	200
Bread	50
Milk (Cow's)	400 ml
Vegetables	500
Fruits	200
Sago	100
Egg	One
Oil	10
Sugar	30
Tea or coffee	7

This diet provides

Calories	2100
Protein	55 g
Fat	36 g

Some common foodstuffs with low amounts of purine are listed in the following table. These can be used in formulating low purine diets.

FOODS WITH INSIGNIFICANT AMOUNT OF PURINE

Vegetables	Cereals	Miscellaneous
Beetroot	Maize	Butter, oil
Brinjal	Rice	Cheese
Cabbage	Wheat	Cream
Calabash cucumber		Egg
Carrot		Fruits of all kinds
Cucumber		Gelatin
Ladies fingers		Milk
Lettuce		Nuts
Potato		Sugar and Sweets
Pumpkin	Tapioca	
Tomato	Yeast	
Turnips		

LOW PHENYLALANINE DIETS

These diets are deficient in most of the nutrients. They can be used for children of 6-12 months old (diet A) and 2-3 years old) (diet B) suffering from Phenyl ketonosis. The younger children should be getting breast milk in addition to the diet:

Principle

The following foods should be avoided while formulating the diet:

1. Wheat, bajra, barley, jowar and maize.
2. Redgram dal, horse gram, rajmah, Bengal gram whole
3. a) Agathi, bottle gourd leaves, carrot leaves, Fenugreek leaves, pumpkin leaves, spinach, tamarind leaves

   b) Colocasia, yam, tender jack

4. Almonds, gingelly seeds, groundnuts
5. Hen egg, cow's milk, curd, cheese

Foodstuffs	Diet A	Diet B
Age of child	6-12 months old	2-3 years old
	g	g
Rice	50	100
Dal	15	20
Vegetables	100	200
Fruits	100	100
Milk (Buffalo)	100 ml	100 ml
Sago or Arrow root	50	50
Sugar	10	20
Oil	10	20

These diets provide

Calories	800	1125
Protein	13.6 g	22.3 g
Phenylalanine	235 mg	348 mg

LOW PROTEIN, LOW CARBOHYDRATE AND LOW SODIUM DIET

This diet provides less protein, carbohydrate and sodium than recommended. It can be used for a diabetic patient who is suffering from acute glomerulonephritis or uraemia and has high blood pressure.

Principle

The following foods are avoided while formulating the diet:

1. Sugar, sweets, puddings, chocolates, preserves

2. Salt in cooking or on table
3. Roots and tubers like potato, sweet potato, beetroot, yam, colocasia
4. Dried fruits and nuts
5. Fruits like banana, sapota, custard apple
6. Sea fish, salted meat, salted dry fish, liver
7. All foods to which salt or baking soda has been added in cooking
8. Salted butter and cheese
9. Pickles and chutneys
10. Alcoholic beverages

Sample diet

Foodstuffs	Amount (g)
Sago or arrow root	150
Rice or atta	100
Pulses	15
Vegetables	400
Milk	50 ml
Orange or sweet lime	200
Oil	35

This diet provides

Calories	1500
Protein	27 g
Fat	40 g
Carbohydrate	260 g
Sodium	0.3 g

LOW COPPER DIET

This diet is as close to normal diet as possible. It is adequate in almost all nutrients. It can be used for children of 4-6 years suffering from Wilson's diseases or hepato-lenticular degeneration. A list of foods which are low in copper content is given and diets can be formulated with the help of these foods.

Principle

The following foods should be avoided while formulating such diets.

1. Spices
2. Roots and tubers except given in the list
3. Vegetables except given in the list
4. Leafy vegetables except given in the list
5. Nuts
6. Organ meats and shell fish
7. Mushrooms
8. Bran
9. Chocolates
10. Whole grain cereals and legumes
11. Copper cooking vessels
12. If water contains more than 1 ppm of cu, it should be distilled and used.

Sample diet

Foodstuffs	Amount	Foodstuffs	Amount
Polished rice	150 g	Vegetables	150 g
Refined wheat flour	100 g	Fruits	100 g
Dal	25 g	Milk	400 ml
Green leafy vegetables	25 g	Sugar	30 g
Roots and tubers	25 g	Oil	20 g

This diet provides:

Calories	1700	Fat	40 g
Protein	45 g	Copper	1.00 mg

Note: Copper value of milk is not available, hence it has not been included.

VEGETABLE EXCHANGE A

These vegetables may be used as desired. Carbohydrates and calories are negligible.

Leafy vegetables	Other vegetables
Amaranth	Ash gourd
Bathuya	Bitter gourd
Brussels sprouts	Brinjal
Cabbage	Calabash cucumber
Celery	Cauliflower
Coriander leaves	Cho-Cho (Marrow)
Curry leaves	Cucumber
Fenugreek leaves	Drumstick
Lettuce	French beans
Mint	Khol-Khol
Rape leaves	Ladies-fingers
Spinach	Mango, green
Soya leaves	Onion stalks
	Parwar
	Plantain flower
	Pumpkin
	Radish
	Rhubarb stalks

Leafy vegetables	*Other vegetables*
	Ridge gourd
	Snake gourd
	Tinda
	Tomato, green
	Turnip

VEGETABLE EXCHANGE B

Carbohydrates-10 g **Calories- 50**

Root vegetables	Quantity (g)
Beetroot	75
Carrot	105
Colocasia	45
Onion (medium)	90
Potato	45
Sweet potato	30
Tapioca	30
Yam (elephant)	60
Yam	45
Other vegetables	
Artichoke	60
Broad beans	90
Cluster beans	90
Double beans	50
Jack, tender	105
Jackfruit seeds	30

Root vegetables	Quantity (g)
Leeks	60
Peas	45
Plantain, green	75
Singhara	45

FRUIT EXCHANGE

Carbohydrates-10 g **Calories- 50**

Fruit	Quantity g	Approximate No. or size g
Amla	90	20 medium
Apple	75	1 small
Banana	30	¼ medium
Cape gooseberry	150	40 small
Cashew fruit	90	2 medium
Custard apple	50	¼
Dates	30	3
Figs	135	6 medium
Grapes	105	20
Grape fruit	150	½ big
Guava	100	1 medium
Jack fruit pieces	60	3 medium
Jambu fruit	50	10 big
Lemon	90	1 medium
Loquat	105	6 big

Fruit	Quantity *g*	Approximate *No. or size g*
Mango	90	1 small
Mangosteen	75	2 medium
Melon	270	¼ medium
Orange	90	1 small
Papaya	120	2 medium
Peach	135	1 medium
Pear	90	1 medium
Pineapple	90	1 medium
Plum	120	4 medium
Pomegranate	75	1 small
Strawberry	105	40
Sweet lime	150	1 medium
Tomato	240	4 medium
Water melon	175	¼ small

CEREAL EXCHANGE

30 g provide Calories: 100

Carbohydrates: 20 g; Protein: 2 g

Bajra	Rice flakes
Barley	Rice puffed
Bread	Sago*
Cholam (jowar)	Samai
Corn flakes	Semolina (Suji)
Maize, dry	Vermicelli (Savian)
Oatmeal	Wheat flour

Ragi
Rice
Wheat, broken (dalia)
White flour

To meet carbohydrates and calories add 5 g. sugar

*Requires supplementation with other high protein foods, when used.

LEGUME AND PULSE EXCHANGE

30 g provide Calories: 100:
Carbohydrates: 15g; Protein: 6 g

Bengal gram
Bengal gram, roasted
Besan (Bengal gram flour)
Black gram
Cow gram
Green gram
Horse gram
Kabuli Channa (White gram)
Lentils
Moth beans
Peas, dried
Rajmah
Rawan
Red gram

FLESH FOOD EXCHANGE

Calories: 70; Protein: 10 g

Food	Quantity (g)
Beef	60
Crab	120 Nos.
Egg, duck*	2 Nos.
Egg, hen*	2 Nos.
Fish, big	60
Fish, small	60
Fish, Vajra	60
Fowl	60

Food	Quantity (g)
Liver, sheep	60
Mutton muscle	60
Pigeon	50
Pork	60
Prawn	60

*Provides 100 calories.

MILK EXCHANGE

Calories: 100; Protein: 5 g.

Food	Quantity
Butter milk	750 ml
Cheese	30 g
Curd	210 g
Khoa	30 g
Milk, Buffalo	90 ml
Milk, Cow	180 ml
Food	*Quantity*
Milk, Skimmed*	260 ml
Milk, Skimmed, powder*	30 g

* Provides 10 g, protein

FAT EXCHANGE

Calories: 100; Fat: 11 g

Food	Quantity (g)
Almonds	15
Butter	15

Food	Quantity (g)
Cashewnuts	20
Coconut	30
Ghee	11
Groundnuts roasted	20
Hydrogenated fat (vanaspati)	11
Oil (coconut, mustard)	11
Pistachionut	15
Walnuts	15

EXCHANGE LIST FOR COOKED FOODS

Weight and volume per serving cooked (providing 100 Cals.) for diabetic patients

	Weight (g)	Volume
Cereal exchange		
Boiled rice	100	1 K
Jowar roti	55	½
Phulka	44	1½
Bread	40	2 slices
Pulse exchange		
Bengal gram dal	94	¾ K
Cuddy	140	1 K
Rajmah	100	¾ K
Green gram whole	150	1K
Sambar	120	¾ K

	Weight (g)	Volume
Vegetable exchange		
Brinjal bhurtha	100	3/4K
Ridge gourd curry	155	1 K
Fried dondakai	138	11/4 K
Char chori	110	1 K
Kootu	116	¾ K
Matar paneer	105	¾ K
Palak wali dal	140	1 K
Snack exchange		
Basen ka pura	50	½
Dahi vadai	96	2
Dosai	32	¾
Idli	85	1½
Kodai shooter kachori	23	½
Poha	50	½
Sago vadai	30	1
Sandwich	33	1
Upma	64	½ K

Note: K-Katori or Bowl: Volume 150 ml.

RECIPES

Cereal exchange

1. Boiled Rice (ragi and broken wheat)

Ingredients	*Weight (gm)*	*Volume*
Rice	200	1½ K
Water	450 ml	3 K

Water for ragi and broken wheat	600-800 ml	4-5 K
Weight for cooked rice	620 g	
Volume of cooked rice	6 katories	

2. ***Phulka***

Ingredients	*Weight (gm)*	*Volume*
Wheat flour	200	21/4 K
Water	100 ml	¾ K
Weight of phulkas	280 g	
No. of phulkas	8	

3. ***Jowar Roti (Makki roti, Ragi roti)***

Ingredients	*Weight (gm)*	*Volume*
Jowar atta	200	21/4 K
Water	150 ml	1 K
Salt	to taste	
Weight of Roti	250 g	
No. of roties	One	

Pulse exchange

1. Bengal gram dal (Black gram dal, green gram dal, lentil dal and red gram dal)

Ingredients	Weight (gm)	Volume
Dal	100	¾ K
Oil/ghee	15	4 tsp
Water	450 ml	3 K
Spices	as required	
Weight of cooked al	625 g	

Volume of cooked dal 5 Katories

2. *Cuddy*

Ingredients	*Weight (gm)*	*Volume*
Bengal gram dal flour (Basen)	200	2½ K
Curd	500	4½ K
Onion	200	Four
Water	as required	
Oil	75	15 tsp
Spices	as required	
Weight of cuddy	2250 g	
Volume of cooked cuddy	18 katories	

3. *Rajmah (Rawan, Kale chole)*

Ingredients	*Weight (gm)*	*Volume*
Rajmah	200	2K
Onion	100	2 medium size
Tomato	100	2
Oil	30	6 tsp
Ginger	10	a small piece
Garlic	5	5 pods
Coriander leaves	1	a small bunch
Spices	as required	
Weight of cooked Rajmah	948 g	
Volume of cooked Rajmah	17 katories	

4. *Green gram whole (Black gram whole, lentil whole)*

Ingredients	Weight (g)	Volume
Green gram wholeq200	13/4L\K	

Green chillies	5	Three
Ginger	3	a small piece
Ghee or butter	20	5 tsp
Water	900 ml	6 K
Spices	as required	
Weight of cooked dal	1120 g	
Volume of cooked dal	8 katories	

5. Sambar

Ingredients	*Weight (g)*	*Volume*
Red gram dal	200	1½K
Onion	50	1 medium size
Oil	10	2 tsp
Curry leaves	1	a few
Water	900 ml 6 katories	
Spices	as required	
Weight of cooked sambar	1220 g	
Volume of cooked sambar	8 katories	

Vegetable exchange

1. Brinjal Bhurtha

Ingredients	*Weight (gm)*	*Volume*
Big round brinjals	200	One
Onions	100	2 medium size
Tomato	50	One
Green chillies	3	Two
Coriander leaves	a few	
Oil	20	5 tsp

Spices	as required	
Weight of cooked Bhurtha	212 g	
Volume of cooked Bhurtha	2 Katories	

2. *Ridge gourd curry* (*Calabash cucumber, tinda and pumpkin*)

Ingredients	*Weight (g)*	*Volume*
Ridge gourd	200	Three
Onions	50	One medium size
Tomato	30	¾
Oil	10	2 tsp
Spices	as required	
Weight of cooked ridge gourd	217 g	
Volume of cooked ridge gourd	1½ katories	

3. Fried Dondakai

Ingredients	*Weight (g)*	*Volume*
Dondakai	200	25
Onion	30	One small
Oil	10	2 tsp
Spices	as required	
Weight of cooked Dondakai	150 g	
Volume of cooked Dondakai	1¼ katories	

4. Char Chori

Ingredients	*Weight (g)*	*Volume*
Cabbage	50	¼ of small cabbage
Potato	50	One small
Spinach	50	Two bundles (small)
Cauliflower	50	One big piece

Ingredients	Weight (g)	Volume
Radish	25	¼
Peas	50	3 tbsp
Brinjal	50	Two small
Pumpkin	50	1 small piece
Punch foran	5	1 tsp
Ingredients	*Weight (g)*	*Volume*
Green chillies	10	6
Jaggery	10	a small piece
Mustard oil	20	4 tsp
Turmeric	a pinch	
Salt	to taste	
Water	as required	

Weight of cooked char chori430 g

Vol. of cooked char chori4 katories

5. *Kootu*

Ingredients	*Weight (gm)*	*Volume*
Bengal gram dal	100	¾ K
Calabash cucumber	300	½ of small calabash cucumber
Green chillies	7	Five
Coconut (fresh)	50	¼
Oil	10	2 tsp

Weight of cooked kootu 825 g

Volume of cooked kootu51/4 katories

6. *Matar Panir*

Ingredients	*Weight (gm)*	*Volume*
Peas (shelled)	250	2½ K

Panir	100	10 pieces (medium size)
Onion	50	One
Tomato	25	One small
Oil	15	4 tsp
Ginger	2	a small piece
Water	300 ml	2 K
Green coriander leaves	a few leaves	
Weight of cooked matar panir	638 g	
Volume of matar panir	4½ katories	

7. Palak wali dal

Ingredients	*Weight (gm)*	*Volume*
Green gram dal	50	1/3 K
Spinach	250	10 small bundles
Green chillies	5	Two
Onion	15	½
Tomato	30	One
Oil	25	5 tsp
Water	150 ml	1 K
Spices	as required	
Weight of cooked palak dal	525 g	
Vol. of cooked palak dal	4 katories	

Snack exchange

1. Basen ka pura (Pesarattu)

Ingredients	*Weight (gm)*	*Volume*
Bengal gram dal flour (Basen)	200	21/3
Onions	75	Two

Tomato	100	Three
Green chillies	5	Four
Green coriander leaves	3	1 bunch
Water	450 ml	3 K
Oil	60	15 tsp
Salt	to taste	
Weight of total pura	607 g	
Volume of total pura	6	

2. *Dahi Vadai or Chat (Northern)*

Ingredients	*Weight (gm)*	*Volume*
Green gram dal	100	¾ K
Black gram dal	100	¾ K
Oil (absorbed)	73	½ K
Curd	1325	12 K
Jaggery	100	10 tbsp
Tamarind	100	½ K
Red chillie powder	10	2 tsp
Roasted cumin powder	10	2 tsp
Garam masala	5	1 tsp
Kala namak	3	½ tsp
Salt	to taste	
Weight of chat	2530 g	
Total No. of vadai	66	

3. *Dosai*

Ingredients	*Weight (gm)*	*Volume*
Rice	75	½ K
Parboiled rice	75	½ K

Black gram dal	50	1/3 K
Oil	23	6 tsp
Salt	to taste	
Weight of cooked dosai	295 g	
No. of dosai	Seven	

4. *Idli*

Ingredients	*Weight (gm)*	*Volume*
Parboiled rice	150	1K
Black gram dal	50	1/3 K
Salt	to taste	
Weight of cooked idlies	512 g	
No. of total idlies	Nine	

5. *Kodai shooter kachori (Kachori)*

Ingredients	*Weight (gm)*	*Volume*
Fresh peas	125	1K
White flour	140	2 K
Vanaspati	20	5 tsp
Mustard Oil	80	16 tsp
Chillie powder	2	½ tsp
Sugar	10	2 tsp
Cumin powder	2	½ tsp
Asafetida	¼	a very small pinch
Salt	to taste	
Water	as required	
Weight of kachori	365g	
No. of kachori	Eight	

6. *Poha (Awal)*

Ingredients	*Weight (gm)*	*Volume*
Pressed rice	200	2 K
Oil	40	8 tsp
Peas (shelled)	75	¾ K
Onion	150	4
Green chillies	10	8
Green coriander	5	a few leaves
Coconut scrapings	50	5 tbsp
Turmeric	a pinch	
Lime juice	10 ml	½ lime
Mustard	a pinch	
Salt	to taste	
Water	as required	
Sugar (optional)	7	1½ tsp
Weight of cooked poha	900 g	
Volume of total poha	9 katories	

7. *Sago vadai*

Ingredients	*Weight (gm)*	*Volume*
Sago	215	1½ K
Potato	500	12
Oil (absorbed)	160	32 tsp
Groundnuts (Roasted)	70	½ K
Green chillies	15	12
Salt	to taste	
Weight of sago vadai	865 g	
No. of sago vadai	32	

8. *Sandwiches*

Ingredients	*Weight (g)*	*Volume*
Bread	80	4 slices
Butter	25	4 tsp
Tomato	40	1 big
Black pepper	½	a small pinch
Salt	½ a small pinch	
Mustard powder	½	a small pinch
Weight of the sandwiches	125 g	
No. of sandwiches	Four	

9. *Upma*

Ingredients	*Weight (g)*	*Volume*
Semolina (Suji)	120	1 K
Green chillies	3	2
Mustard	2	a pinch
Ginger	2 a small piece	
Onion	40	2 small
Curry leaves	1	6
Oil	25	5 tsp
Cashewnuts	20	4-6
Water	375 ml	2½ K
Black gram dal	5	1½ tsp
Bengal gram dal	5	11/4 tsp
Salt	-	to taste
Lime juice	5	1 tsp
Weight of total cooked upma	505 g	
Volume of upma	4 katories	

FOODS RICH IN OXALIC ACID

Horse gram	Rhubarb (stalk)
Khesari dal	Almonds
Amaranth, tender	Cashewnuts
Curry leaves	Garden cress seeds
Drumstick leaves	Gingelly seeds
Gogu (*pitwa* or *ambadi*)	Amla
Mustard leaves, tender	Phalsa
Neem leaves, tender	Wood apple
Paruppu Kerai (*kulfa*)	Bhangari
Spinach	Chookri-ka-atta
Tamarind leaves, tender	Chookri-ka-patla
Drumstick leaves	Ripe chillies
Lotus stem, dry	Coca
Plantain flower	Tea
Plantain, green	

FOODS WHICH CONTAIN LOW AMOUNTS OF COPPER

Cereals	*Pulses*	*Vegetables*
Refined wheat flour	Green gram dal	Broad beans
Polished rice	Red gram dal	Jackfruit seeds
Maida	Dried peas	Lotus stem
Jowar		Pink beans
Maize		Plantain flower
		Tinda
		Tomato
		Vegetable marrow

Green leafy vegetables	Fruits
Lettuce	Amla
Celery leaves	Apricot
Brussels sprouts	Bilimbi
	Cape gooseberry
	Lemon sweet
	Lichi
	Malta
	Loquat
	Melon
	Melon water
	Papaya
	Peaches
	Pears
	Phalsa
	Plums
	Tomato

Average nutritive value of foodstuffs per 100 g.

Foodstuffs	Protein g	Fat g	CHO g	Calories Kcal	Calcium mg	Phosphorous mg	Iron mg	Carotene ug	Thiamin mg	Riboflavin mg	Niacin mg	Vit. C mg	Pyridoxine mg
1. Cereals	9.9	2.3	71.0	344	79.8	277.3	5.6	56.7	0.34	0.17	2.42	-	0.32
2. Bread	7.8	0.7	51.9	245	11.0	-	1.1	-	0.07	-	0.70	-	0.30
3. Biscuit Salt	6.6	32.4	54.6	534	-	-	-	-	-	-	-	-	-
4. Biscuit Sweet	6.4	15.2	71.9	450	-	-	-	-	-	-	-	-	-
5. Pulses	22.6	2.0	58.4	342	121.1	337.7	7.3	96.1	0.47	0.21	2.35	0.60	0.50
6. Roots and tubers	1.2	0.2	16.0	70	37.7	90.4	0.9	222.3	0.05	0.05	0.54	14.25	0.35
7. Other vegetables	2.2	0.3	6.3	36	42.2	51.0	1.7	98.5	0.08	0.05	0.44	27.80	-
8. Nuts and oilseeds	15.2	46.6	20.4	578	258.0	464.0	6.0	31.4	0.44	0.28	4.03	0.82	-
9. Coconut Milk	3.4	41.0	11.9	430	15.0	140.0	1.6	-	0.08	0.04	0.60	3.00	-
10. Coconut water	1.4	0.1	4.4	24	24.0	10.0	0.1	-	0.10	-	0.10	2.00	-
11. Fruits	1.1	0.4	7.6	79	36.2	34.0	1.8	294.0	0.06	0.12	0.40	45.10	0.15
12. Meat	21.0	4.9	0.8	131	134.2	245.7	1.3	9.0	0.05	0.10	2.11	3.63	-
13. Egg	13.3	13.3	-	173	60.0	220.0	2.1	420.0	0.10	0.40	0.10	-	0.19
14. Milk	3.6	5.8	4.7	85	166.7	113.3	0.2	50.0	0.04	0.34	0.16	1.33	-
15. Curd	3.1	4.0	3.0	60	149.0	93.0	0.2	31.0	0.05	0.16	0.10	1.00	-

16. Butter	-	81.0	-	729	-	-	-	960.0	-	-	-	-	-
17. Ghee	-	100.0	-	900	-	-	-	600.0	-	-	-	-	- -
18. Oil	-	100.0	-	900	-	-	-	-	-	-	-	-	-
19. Sugar	0.1	-	99.4	398	12.0	1.0	-	-	-	-	-	-	-
20. Honey	0.3	-	79.5	319	5.0	16.0	0.9	-	-	0.04	0.20	4.00	-
21. Jaggery	0.4	0.1	95.0	383	80.0	40.0	11.4	168.0	0.02	0.04	0.50	-	-
22. Sago	0.2	0.2	87.1	351	10.0	10.0	1.3	-	0.01	-	0.20	-	-
23. Nutrinuggets	82.2	-	-	862	-	-	-	-	-	-	-	-	-
24. Spert	23.0	1.0	70.0	381	-	-	-	750.0	1.50	1.80	32.00	38.00	3.60
25. Green leafy vegetables	3.8	0.6	6.0	45	295.8	64.2	11.9	4390.3	0.09	0.22	1.30	65.87	0.22
26. Condiments and spices	9.8	6.6	40.6	261	410.3	239.8	14.5	241.2	0.20	0.19	1.59	15.13	-

* These values represent ug of vitamin A.

Courtesy: NIN, Hyderabad, India.

12

Tracking a Food Trend

Just as we are getting used to new American and European menus featuring hickory-smoked lobster, fresh New Jersey-tomato sherbet, and black cherry balsamic compote, someone tells us it is time for a change!

Not long ago, for example, well-known French Chef Pierre Franey declared in the New York Times, that he was experiencing a powerful yearning lately for hearty, classic French fare (as in the roast chicken and mashed potatoes)

Almost simultaneously, a leading Manhattan Chef/ Restaurateur, Jonathan Waxman, and his partner announced the opening of their third restaurant, this one specialising in hearty, classic country French fare.

Coincidence or conspiracy? Or put in another way: How exactly do food trends evolve?

Trends can be a single item (say, wild mushrooms), a type of food (exotic produce) a style of cooking (nouvelle or new American), or a philosophy (healthful cuisine). Trend has "legs" it becomes an established part of culinary culture.

Pasta, for example, is versatile, cheap, and nutritious enough to have become an international best seller, and most decent restaurant, catering, and "delis" around the world, now offer a selection of cold pasta salads, and pasta dishes.

A mere 10 years ago, a group of innovative Italian restauraterus on the East and West American coast began importing and serving a bitter red lettuce called Radicchio. Now it is garnishing room service trays around the country.

A couple of years ago, Stephen Pyles, co-owner and Chef of the highly regarded Routh Street Café in Dallas, "played around" with smoke-cooking vegetables. Other Chefs used this around the world.

Same stories with "Junk fish". Americans' interest in healthful eating has created a demand for fresh fish at inexpensive and moderately priced restaurants. "Now fishermen get $5 a pound for stuff, that a few years ago, they would have thrown back into the water".

And what for the future?

World-renowned restaurateurs and Chefs have observed food trends for the last 20 years and states "superficial fashion and tricky arrangements and structures" are over.

KEY CONCEPTS FOUND IN CURRENT CUISINE TRENDS

- Local products
- Regional cooking
- Adjust to the season and marketplace
- Simplify menu- procedures- service
- Reduce preparation time
- Remember nutritional aspects
- Avoid thick sauces
- Experiment
- Use today's technology
- Use skills, not gimmicks
- Remember to provide the correct price/value for your market

OPERATION MANAGEMENT IV

Purchasing

Introduction

Good, professional purchasing skill is the key to dispose of certain items

- At the right time
- With the right quality
- With the right quantity
- In optimal condition for use
- At an interesting price
- At the right place

Optimizing purchasing is to contribute on a significant way to the good work process. It is the first decisive step to a correct and good "mise en place" and should not be left to chance.

Purchasing is influenced by numerous parameters.

- Merchandise knowledge
- Quality and hygiene
- Quantity
- Manpower
- Storage
- Storage facilities
- Ordering system

PURCHASING FACTORS

- Establishment offer	=	Menu, "a la carte"
- Recipes	=	
- Ordering system	=	Telephone order, etc.
- Quantity	=	

- Geographical site = Mountain, city, resort
- Storage facilities = Storeroom refrig/Dry store and Nalkin.
- Purchasing facilities = Market, delivery, etc.
- Style of establishment = Pizzeria, 5 stars hotel, etc
- Equipment = Combo-cooker, others
- Manpower = Qualified, non-qualif.
- Merchandise knowledge = Tests
  - Sales prices

MERCHANDISE KNOWLEDGE

A good purchasing manager must imperatively have ample knowledge of merchandises. That is obviously including broad information and contacts with the different market and suppliers, to be always on top of changes and new products.

That should translate into receiving salesmen, visit industrials, be in specialised national and international fairs, comparing price lists, having some exchanges with colleagues, permanent training, participation in congress, etc.

The offer has never been so vast as nowadays. The Chef must make a good choice among the multitude of products. Merchandise testing is an important help. This starts with fresh supplies. For example: a carrot cake is much better if carrots have a natural sugar content instead of being sour.

The more an establishment has the use of intermediary products or convenience food, the more products must be tasted rigorously and systematically before purchasing large quantities.

It is always beneficial to test and taste the largest number of supplies in the market:

For example, portioned marmalade.

1. Ask your providers to supply samples of their portioned marmalade of all sorts.

2. One day, (it would be ridiculous to have sample tasting on different days) have a sample taste with your manager, the purchasing agent and a maximum of persons to sample the product.
3. Make a comparative-tasting taking in account everybody's opinion
4. Chose the ones that have made the most points among this crowd.

The chosen products should stay in the assortment for a while since recipes and working schedules have been accorded with the products.

Since product tasting take a good amount of time, it is necessary to prepare it well. The test results must be written on a test sheet and kept to consult at all time.

Criteria

- Colour
- Conservation
- Modification during cooking process
- Aptitude to microwave
- Aptitude to freezing
- Aptitude to heat
- Consistency
- Texture
- Flavour and odour

Flavour and Odour

Those are probably the most important. It is necessary, that the person that participate to the food tasting, are knowledgeable in term of culinary perception.

Quality and Hygiene

Quality has an incidence on purchasing, especially during the process of choosing suppliers and food producers. Latest are not always apt to produce the same quality for different product.

Taking in account frozen goods, everybody knows that there are big differences in quality. Some firms are recognized to produce high quality and expensive items.

Others are recognized to produce lower quality at better prices. Buying expensive or inexpensive depend, indeed of the financial capacity and the market we are catering for.

However, there is one factor that we always have to take into account when purchasing:

- The supreme condition is buying and preparing only merchandises of irreproachable hygienic quality, federal laws are monitoring hygienic rules that have to be followed to the point.
- A professional has to be fully aware of its responsibility toward guests and patrons. Never play with your clients' health with meals of a questionable hygienic origin.
- Never purchase doubtful products to save on food cost.

During conceptual plans of a kitchen, the architect, the builder and the kitchen Chef should always team-up to design the project, to obtain maximal results.

They should work together on size of working areas, size of operating equipment and machinery, electrical installation points, water connection to harmonise, rationalise and facilitate later production, which at the end of the day, will make the kitchen a profit centre or a total disaster.

KITCHEN LAYOUT

Not only culinary knowledge but the layout of the production kitchen is important. Here is a geographical view of a well-designed kitchen.

- Chef and sous chef office
- Showers
- Staff cantin

- Locker room
- Cold kitchen, vegetable, salads
- Preparation
- Main kitchen
- Butchery
- Fishery
- Pastry
- Pot cleaning area
- Control
- Cold rooms
- Freezers
- Store room
- Store room office
- Dishwashing areas
- Toilets

In large kitchen more locals will be added such as staff kitchen, special regimen kitchen, etc.

STYLES OF CUISINES

An analysis will determine the style of cooking according to:

- Clientele
- Layout of the establishment
- Size of establishment
- Choice of meals offered
- Style and volume of establishment
- Style of service

Differences are to be made between:

Conventional cuisine

Production and finishing are made in the same kitchen

Production kitchen and combined finishing

Production and finishing are made separately

Production kitchen and separated finishing (satellite kitchen)

Satellite kitchen separated from the main producing kitchen. Well organized you can serve a lot of dishes in a short period of time.

Fast food kitchen

Installed in such a way to maximize fast service. Generally using pre-prepared or finished goods at low cost. Staff is generally trained for a specific task, no need for high professional. Everything is installed for a non-demanding clientele.

Open kitchen

Could be called show kitchen, finishing and preparation is made in front of patrons.

Experimental kitchen

For research and development, usually made for food service companies.

It is a study place to experiment on conservation or to create new flavour, does not produce for customers.

Kitchen Installation

Cooking equipment

Modern technology is changing constantly, always growing market represent a real challenge for modern cooks.

Here is an important list of kitchen equipment:

- Cooking and roasting oven
- Rotisserie
- Pressure braising device
- Pressure steam pot
- Fryer

- Vitro-ceramic cooker
- Grill
- Charcoal grill
- Induction cooking device
- Cooking pot marmite
- Combined roast and steam oven
- Combined steamer
- Induction oven
- Microwave oven
- Traditional combined gas and electric stove
- Low cooking oven
- Pizza oven
- Salamander

Automate for cooking

In large establishment the use of automate cooking, permits on the long run to produce more without the need of adding more staff.

- Autoclave
- Automatic oven
- Roasting automate
- Steam automate
- Frying automate
- Boiling automate
- Regenerating equipment

To cook foods we are using four styles of heat transmitter:

1. Heat by contact (i.e. grilled steak)
2. Heat by transmission (i.e. fries)
3. Heat by radiation (i.e. salamander)
4. Combined heat (i.e. oven)

COOKING KITCHEN UTENSILS

Today, we are disposing of a vast range of form and material.

Stainless steel

The most used material. It does not rust and is very strong.

Advantages: Insensitive to acids and salt, solid, neutral to smell and taste, very economical.

Inconveniences: Heavy for large size pan and casserole, heat transmission not optimal.

Aluminium

Advantages: It does not rust, good heat transmitter, cheap, goes well to cook with gas.

Inconveniences: soft material, sensible to acids, white sauces and soups become greyish when stirred, welded handles get easily damaged.

Copper

Advantages: Does not rust, very good heat transmitter, good regulation of heat allowing it to be non-stick.

Inconveniences: verdigris's formation if insufficient layer of tin plate, hard and long cleaning process, maintenance cost elevated (coat of tin plate), destruction of vital vitamin C.

Silver (silverware for service)

Advantages: Give a luxurious look to any table

Inconveniences: long maintenance procedure, not apt to every ailment

Synthetic material

Advantages: Light, very easy to maintain, cheap, not noisy at handling.

Inconveniences; Sensible to acids, sensible to excessive heating

Glass and porcelain

Advantages: Insensible to salt and acids, good heat resistance, give a good visibility during cooking process.

Inconveniences: Breakable, bad heat conductor

LIGHT KITCHEN EQUIPMENT

Again, thanks to technology those robots allow us to save a lot of time in our kitchen, by doing menial jobs.

Few examples of light kitchen equipment:

- Slicing machine
- Cutter
- Dishwashing machine
- Vegetable washing device
- Cream beater
- Mincer, shopper
- Mixer
- Dough stirrer
- Robot coupe
- Vacuum pack machine
- Kitchen scales

KITCHEN TOOLS

Good kitchen tools are imperative and are a question of honour for professionals. Most of the Chefs and cooks agree on this point and they are normally buying their own working tools. Culinary staffs get accustomed to it, as it is corresponding to each one way of work.

Few examples of kitchen tools.

- Boning knife
- Carving spoon (Parisienne)
- Butcher knife
- Chef knife
- Bread knife
- Fish scale knife
- Fish serving fork
- Fish scissors
- Carving knife
- Meat serving fork
- Bone saw
- Kitchen knife
- Slicing knife
- Moulds
- Potato peeler
- Lemon knife
- Rind knife
- Spatulas
- Potato baking spoon
- Office knife
- Etc.

GASTRONORM

A very important kitchen tool and practical concept. This is the standardisation of kitchen containers according to international norms of gastronomy and the DIN 66075.

From merchandise's receiving to storage, cold and hot preparation, cooking, and distribution, those standardized containers are used at all level and can be used for transportation, processing, oven cooking, refrigeration, freezing, and serving. With this system we obtain maximum efficiency, thus obtaining better benefits.

Advantages:

1. Stackable
2. Waterproof (thanks to special lid system)
3. Edges solidified by special treatment
4. Security handles
5. All usual sizes available
6. All usual depth available

3. Kitchen Brigade

This is where you can really admire the master of the place, real shining "star" among his troop of collaborators. But TEAMWORK is essential and should be written in majuscule in all kitchens around the world. There is not good Chef without good team. It does also mean that hierarchy must exist, since the Chef is responsible for all stage of work distribution and final quality.

The importance and size of a kitchen brigade depends on:

- Style of establishment
- Size of establishment
- Installations
- Organisation
- Staffing guide (auxiliary staff, staff in formation or staff having finished their apprenticeship)
- Choice of meals

As principle we are distinguishing three kind of brigade

- Small kitchen brigade (until 7 professional cooks)
- Medium kitchen brigade (at least 8 professional cooks)
- Large kitchen brigade (at least 15 professional cooks)

Functions

In a large professional kitchen brigade, responsibilities are shared as follow:

- **Kitchen director**: Chef in charge of all kitchens. Kitchen Chefs are under his authority.
- **Kitchen chef**: Is responsible for the kitchen and the brigade
- **Sous chef**: Replace Kitchen Chef during absence and take over responsibility
- **Kitchen chef assistant**: Carry out all administrative work for the Kitchen Chef
- **Chef de partie**: Cook in charge of one specific area
- **Saucier**: Is responsible for the preparation of stocks, bases and sauces for meat, fish, poultry, games. In large brigade you will find a "saucier", a "rotisseur" or a "poissonier". Normally, in small and middle size brigade, you will not find a "sous Chef" and the "Chef saucier" will be the kitchen Chef's deputy.
- **The Rotisseur**: Is responsible for dishes with fish, meat, poultry, vegetable, game prepared according to the following bases
    - Oven roasting and skewer
    - Frying
    - Grilling
- **The Entremetier**: In charge of the preparation of soup, vegetable (to the exception of grilled and fried vegetables prepared by the Rotisseur) as well as pasta, flour, egg and cheese dishes.
- **The grade Manger**: Is responsible for all cold preparation. Its principal tasks are preparation of salads, cold sauces, pates, terrines, galantines, cold dishes, farces, to bone butchery meat, game, fish, crustacean reserved for cooking or roasting.
- **The Pastry Chef**: Is responsible to prepare all hot, cold or iced dessert and sauces accompanying them, all creams and dough for bakery.
- **The Chef Tournant**: Is responsible for replace absent "Chefs de partie" during days off.

- **The Chef de garde**: Is responsible to replace all kitchen work in absence of other cooks.
- **The Dietetic Chef**: Specially trained for diet menus in hospital, or "spa" Hotels. Work with special order from a doctor, special dietetic consideration and collaboration with a diet specialist.
- **Staff cantin Chef**: Is responsible for staff diet and meals. This post exists only in large establishment.
- **The Commis de Cuisine**: are directly subordinates to the "Chefs de partie", they are generally named after the post they are occupying in the kitchen (i.e. commis saucier)
- **The apprentice**: Is learning the trade in 3 years, according to the rules of apprenticeship (in Europe). During his training, he is rotating in each and every kitchen department.

MISE EN PLACE

A magic word and one of the most important:

Means "put in order" and prepare needed working equipment and ingredients. It has to be applied without restriction in all kitchens and all style of cooking.

Example: "Mise en place" for a mayonnaise

Ingredients

- Oil
- Egg yolk
- Mustard
- Vinegar
- Salt pepper

Utensils

- Kitchen bowl
- Whip

All those items must be prepared beforehand to allow this elaboration to be done without interruption. Mayonnaise is a finished product but could be the first step of another preparation.

Example: "Mise en place" for a shrimp cocktail sauce

Ingredients

- Mayonnaise
- Horse radish
- Cognac
- Lemon juice
- Cayenne pepper
- Salt
- White pepper
- Shrimps
- Eggs
- Truffle
- Lemon wedges

Utensils

- Kitchen bowl
- Whip
- Spoon
- Cocktail glasses

This cocktail is again a finished product, but could also be part of another "mise en place", i.e., to be among a buffet with other food items.

Food items, which are part of a "mise en place" may then, include products, which are at different level of food preparation, from the start to the finish.

For the preparation of each dish, it is absolutely necessary to have a precise "mise en place". "Mise en place" of each sequences (breakfast, Lunch, dinner) MUST include all utensils and ingredients needed for the complete elaboration of the menu.

The more precise is the "mise en place", the more it is facilitating service. Precise "mise en place" is creating an easygoing climate in the kitchen.

The expression "A good mise en place is half the work done" can be verified everyday.

The set-up of the "mise en place" will be written by the Chef de cuisine, implemented by the cooks and apprentices, and supervised by each Chef de partie.

For a perfect "mise en place" it is indeed necessary to dispose of a proper supply from storerooms, having a good organisation and planning in the purchasing department.

Steadying, working area before and after service is also part of the "mise en place". Constant supervision of supplies is also part of the "mise en place".

BASE "MISE EN PLACE"

Includes all utensils needed in the kitchen:

- Knifes
- Kitchen bowls
- Trays
- Pots
- Pans
- Aprons
- Cleaning materials
- Cleaning products,
- Etc.

DAILY "MISE EN PLACE"

Is adapted to menus, banquets and daily specialities, etc.

Working area "mise en place"

Specifically adapted to each post (i.e. saucier, butchery, pastry, etc.) and depends indeed of specific tasks for menus, banquets or daily specials.

LATEST FOOD CONCEPTS CHANGES IN EUROPE AND AMERICA

- What is healthier cuisine?
- Healthier ingredient in creative cuisine
- Cholesterol, salt, fat or not?
- Hygiene
- Organic fruits and "veggies" are they just a snobbish trend?
- Profit through new technology and machinery enhancing faster service.
- Consistency in food quality and service

CONTROLLING OUR BUSINESS AND PROFIT THROUGH NEW COMPUTERISED TECHNOLOGY

- Food costing to be perfectly precise = recognizing your profit, knowing where you stand and where exactly you can go.
- Point of sales
- Guest history, why?

Other sources of profit?

- How merchandising can affect our revenues, profit and image?

- Is it necessary to market our concept? Should we wait for the world of mouth?
- Takeaways and home delivery, a good possibility?

Some thoughts on today's competitive edge

- Free market is not a game, it is a war
- In the restaurant industry, you do not sell food and drinks, you are selling a series of services and products.
- Difference is the essence of triumph. Difference is the result of creativity.
- Reaction is the result of retrospection. Pro-action is the result of anticipation.
- Intuition will never replace analysis.
- Managers should always feel the high competition level.
- Good managers do not fall into routine. They are motivating each other.
- Financial statements show the problems, opportunities are found within the market.
- In any change decision, small or important always wonder "what will our customers think?."

Are we customers oriented?

The total quality management quiet revolution

An example of an American & European restaurant's Total Quality Management philosophy

THE "YES ATTITUDE"

- Our rule number 1, is to bring comfort by our service attitude, warm reception, and give the best of ourselves to our guests!

  Our leitmotiv: the "Yes attitude"

We are people of good breeding serving people of good breeding

The following three steps of service and leitmotiv, will be known, owned and implemented at all time by all collaborators.

Our three steps of service

1. A warm and sincere greeting. Use always the guest name, whenever possible
2. Anticipation and Compliance with guest needs
3. Always give fond farewell. Give the guest a warm good-bye and use their names, whenever possible.

Our leitmotiv: The Yes Attitude.

- The X....Restaurant is a place where the genuine care and comfort of our guests is our highest mission.
- We pledge to provide the finest personal service and facilities for our guests, who will always enjoy a warm, relaxed yet refined ambience.
- The X...restaurant experience enlivens the senses, instils well-being, and fulfils even the unexpressed wishes and needs of our guests.

TOTAL QUALITY MANAGEMENT
THE SERVICE MISSION

1. Our leitmotiv will be known, owned and energized by all collaborators.
2. Our motto is "We are people of good breeding serving people of good breeding". We definitely practice teamwork and lateral service to create a positive work environment.
3. All collaborators should practice the three steps of service.

4. All collaborators will successfully complete a training certification to ensure they understand how to perform to the restaurant standards in their position.
5. All collaborators will understand their work area and the established company goals on Food & Beverage covers, and average checks.
6. All collaborators will know the needs of their internal and external customers (employees and guests), so that we may deliver the products and services they expect. Use your contacts with the guests to record and report any specific needs or requests.
7. Each collaborator will continuously identify and report defects throughout the operation.
8. Any collaborator, who receives a customer complaint, "owns "the compliant.
9. Instant guest pacification will be ensured by all. React quickly to correct the problem immediately. Do everything you possibly can to never lose a guest.
10. Guest incident action forms are used to record and communicate every incident of guest dissatisfaction. Every collaborator is empowered to resolve the problem and to prevent a repeat occurrence.
11. Uncompromising levels of cleanliness are the responsibility of very collaborator.
12. "*Smile* - We are on stage". Always maintain positive eye contact. Use the proper vocabulary with our guests. (Use words like "good morning", "I will be happy to"-"my pleasure", etc).

Index

D

E

F

G

N

Q

R

S

T